WordStream

Publishing

ALSO BY MERYL RUNION

Speak Strong
Say what you MEAN. MEAN what you say.
Don't be MEAN when you say it

Power Phrases
The Perfect Words to Say it Right and
Get the Results You Want

Perfect Phrases for Leadership Development
Hundreds of Ready-to-Use Phrases for Guiding
Employees to Reach the Next Level (Perfect Phrases
Series) (w/ Wendy Mack)

Perfect Phrases for Managers and Supervisors, Second
Edition (Perfect Phrases Series)

How To Say It Performance Reviews
(w/ Janelle Brittain)

Perfect Phrases for Managers and Supervisors
Hundreds of Ready-to-Use Phrases for
Any Management Situation

Power Phrases Amplified
Say What You Mean, Mean What You Say,
Get What You Want

How to Restore Sanity
to Our Political Conversations

Reasonable Responses,
Constructive Comebacks
and Powerful Phrases

Meryl Runion

How to Restore Sanity
to Our Political Conversations

Reasonable Responses, Constructive Comebacks and Powerful Phrases

ISBN-13: 978-1-935758-06-8 (paperback format)
ISBN-13: 978-1-935758-05-1 (eBook format)

Editors: Wade Hampton Ryan and Marti Williams
Cover Design: Amanda J. Gargus

Published by:

WordStream Publishing

www.WordStreamPublishing.com

Contents

Foreword
A New Dynamic of Citizen Leadership

There was a time, not too long ago, when one did not share their political opinions in "polite company." However, with the lines between personal information and professional networking increasingly blurred through social networking sites like Facebook and Twitter, we know more about the political beliefs of our family, friends, neighbors and co-workers than ever before.

Furthermore, with our political parties increasingly polarized to "good-versus-evil" talking points, and the news media fueling the flames by putting ratings before reason, the conversations around the dinner table and water cooler are growing increasingly heated.

How to Restore Sanity to Our Political Conversations applies the dynamic leadership approach that I write about in my business books for our political conversations. My business books create leaders at every organizational level. This book creates dynamic citizen leaders at every level, starting with cleaning up our political conversations.

Here's what that means:
1. A Dynamic Citizen Leader is someone who has outgrown all forms of victimhood and tyranny including manipulation and coercive power tactics in favor of the confluence, influence and engagement.
2. A Dynamic Citizen Leader is someone who progressively clarifies and refines their own civil

leadership philosophy and shares it eloquently with others.

3. A Dynamic Citizen Leader is someone who serves community, vision and values instead of personal power needs.

4. A Dynamic Citizen Leader is someone who sees problems and obstacles as invitations to outgrow the perspectives that created them and to embrace higher perspectives to transform them.

5. A Dynamic Citizen Leader is someone who uses Beginner's Mind to obtain fresh perspectives.

6. A Dynamic Citizen Leader is someone who influences others by engaging their higher nature more than by talking.

7. A Dynamic Citizen Leader is someone who progressively clarifies and refines their unique point of view by integrating input from self-reflection, study, mentoring, coaching and feedback.

8. A Dynamic Citizen Leader is someone who doesn't need the word leader in their title to take ownership of their area of influence.

9. A Dynamic Citizen Leader is someone who measures his and other's leadership abilities by their ability to empower others.

10. A Dynamic Citizen Leader is someone who participates in and elevates the national dialogue.

How to Restore Sanity to Our Political Conversations tells you how to be a Dynamic Citizen Leader in your own area of influence, even if that simply means your conversations with the checker at the grocery store. It starts wherever you are, and radiates out.

Introduction
Driving in the political dark

Have you ever faced crazy relatives, offensive coworkers or threatening neighbors? Do any of the following scenarios sound familiar?

> **I was *stunned* into silence**. She didn't just say that, did she? Did she really believe a certain politician was to be feared because he's charismatic and Hitler was charismatic too? Did she honestly expect me to take her argument seriously? It appeared she did.

> **I was *angered* into silence**. When his illogical statement didn't work, he resorted to insults. How dare this longtime friend and associate call me stupid for my considered and well researched comment, spoken in earnest? Did he think that my political opinion justified bullying behavior? It appeared he did.

> **I was *frightened* into silence**. His response sounded threatening. He lived down the street, so perhaps I should just let him rant and not speak. Did he really think people whose yard signs support different views from his are asking to be vandalized? It appeared he did.

If you can relate to any of these scenarios, this book is for you. If you've ever tiptoed around a political discussion at the kitchen table or the water cooler because the very mention of politics brings out the darker side of people, this book is for you. If you ever thought it shouldn't be like this and we ought to and *need* to be able to talk about these things reasonably, this book is for you.

As for me, well, I thank the illogical, ill-mannered and ill-tempered people in my life who motivated me to write this book.

After all, I'm this influential communication speaker and author. I've sold some 400,000 books about how to say things. For me to be silenced by illogical, personal attacks and intimidation is simply not acceptable. These scenarios led me to want to learn how to stop being manipulated by tactics and to stay empowered and coherent in conversations about how we live in the world together (i.e. politics).

I succeeded. Since writing this book, I have learned to move through my anger and fear and to calmly and effectively respond to political idiocy, sideswipes and attacks. It's not that I've learned to tolerate diatribes and blather. I've learned to alchemize it into dialogue.

While I haven't changed the world, I changed *my* world. I learned to gracefully and effectively hold my own. And that influences others. I wrote this book for me, so I could talk to my family, colleagues and coworkers. Then I rewrote it for you, so you can talk to yours.

This book is for YOU.
Okay. Let me be clear. When I say this book is for you, I mean *you*. Even before this book was completed, I got comments like, "I can think of a few people I'd like to send it to." I'm glad people like it, but I much prefer the response to be, "this is something I can use in my own communication."

This book isn't for you to pass on to that "idiot" who is "a few cards short of a full deck." It isn't for the O'Reilly or Beck or Maddow or Olbermann types, or the Obama or Pelosi or Palin types.

It isn't for the kind of lobbyists who define truth based on who signs their checks. (How do they sleep?)

It isn't for power brokers looking to game the system to their advantage and other's disadvantage. (Why do we let them do that?)

It's for you, me, and other citizens who just want to be able to talk about political issues and considerations without needing to take a shower, see a psychiatrist, or visit the emergency room afterwards. It's for those of us who don't want to be complicit by virtue of silence while conscienceless manipulators dominate the national and local political conversation.

Not that activists and professionals can't use this book. After I presented the information here in a keynote to a woman's lobbying group, their subsequent discussion of which initiatives to support went much more smoothly than the previous years' had. So I know this information can make a difference to the sincere pros.

But my main purpose in writing is to pave the way for *you*, so you can talk to your family, neighbors and colleagues about politics. I repeat. This book is for *you*. Not because you're the problem, but because it will help you be part of the solution. Once you've internalized that, I invite you to get copies for others.

Reasonable dialogues do happen

I was shamed into developing these skills by my own pathetic responses. But let's cut ourselves some slack. Where might we have learned to have reasonable political dialogue? On TV? Yeah, right. At school? I laughed out loud when I heard a neighbor boy say to his sister, "You know who's a big fat liar? Obama." And I heard his eight-year-old sister respond:

> *"I don't want to discuss politics with you. I've had enough of those conversations and I'm moving on."*

OMG! Out of the mouths of babes! She's all of eight-years old and she has already learned not to discuss politics! Yes, I was genuinely impressed and I applaud her for not engaging in a win-lose discussion where she no doubt would be the loser. It's a useful phrase to have. However, I'd much rather have heard her say:

> *"Interesting. It sounds like you think Obama is exceptionally dishonest. What does he say or do that leads you to draw that conclusion?"*

So how would we know how to engage in political dialogue when it's a step up to learn how to avoid talking about politics?

Well, reasonable political dialogues are not the norm, but they do happen. I scan the news and blogs to find examples of it so you don't have to. I listen to how people talk politics to uncover those rare times they discuss issues collaboratively, I'm all ears. I pay attention to how they interact when they differ, and contrast that with the contentious communication that seems more common, to expose the mechanics. I study how they handle their differences to add tools to the Sanity Restoration toolbox.

As an American, I find the best examples of reasonable dialogue are more easily discovered overseas. International communities have had to learn how to talk to one another. I do confess that the last time I was overseas, an Australian shoved a newspaper in my face and took me to task for the Iraq war as if I had personally started it. He wasn't ready to exchange ideas for a while. Still, foreign political dialogue often teaches how people can talk to each other about their differences.

The experience of reasonable dialogue is sobering. When you've experienced it, it's harder to go back to the hostile pointless mud-fests. That's why this book isn't just theory. I give my trademark PowerPhrases throughout. The smoke and mirrors, pressuring and manipulative ways we talk about politics creates kind of a stupor. It lulls us into unconsciousness. I wrote to wake me up, and then I rewrote this for *you*.

Waking to and from a nightmare

I immersed myself in the nightmare so you don't have to. Nightmares are especially scary if you don't know you can wake up. Have you ever had this dream?

> You're in danger, but there's nothing you can do. You hit the brakes but the car goes faster. You know there's a road, but all you see is darkness. Is anyone steering?

> Not that you can see! People in the back are oblivious. They're watching an online video of the latest celebutante making a fool of herself. They don't even look up, they call you crazy and they tell you to shut the <bleep> up.

Watching the news or trying to discuss politics could trigger that dream. Learning a better way is the awakening. So I will talk about the nightmare, but unlike some unscrupulous political communicators, I won't stir your fears without offering hope and solutions.

Pinch yourself — you're not just dreaming

What if, politically speaking, we actually are driving in the dark? What if we are racing forward with our headlights turned off? What if you and I unknowingly add to the fog by shutting down or ignoring the very people we need to listen to?

I'm going to tell you something you already know about politics: *Our national political dialogue is insane, ineffective, and destructive.*

Now I'll tell you something you might not have thought about: *That doesn't mean yours has to be.*

In fact, that's all the more reason why you and I need to (take a breath) listen to each other, dialogue instead of debate and sift through the spin together. You know, stop arguing and start communicating about politics. So the next time someone tries to pass nonsense as logic, insults you for disagreeing or pressures you to back down, instead of being stunned into silence or provoked into belligerence, you'll respond with something like:

> *I'm fascinated by your perspective. It's so different from mine. I wonder why we see this so differently.*

You might learn something. Even if you don't, it will sure feel better than being stunned into silence or agitated into your own belligerence.

Meryl Runion

Chapter 1

A simpleton's plea for reasonable dialogue

Some say the court jester had an important role in the King's court. In the guise of a fool, the jester could speak truth that penetrated defenses and hit home without triggering a reaction. Comedians are modern day jesters. Ironically, while posing as simpletons, some political comedians ask the most challenging and insightful questions of their political guests. And while the very serious politician Al Gore wrote a book appealing to the nation to engage in reasonable dialogue, it was a plea from comedian Jon Stewart that had the most impact and stirred the most interest.

A reasonably reasonable appeal for reason

Comedian Jon Stewart made his plea for civilized dialogue in 2004 on the now defunct show *Crossfire*. He asked the show hosts Tucker Carlson and Paul Begala to stop fighting, to stop interviewing knee-jerk reactionary guests who argued unrepresentative extreme positions, to stop allowing emotional provocation to pass for dialogue, to stop trying to win by overpowering, and mainly to stop being part of politicians' divisive strategies. He asked for honest arguments that hold politician's feet to the fire in civilized discourse.

Clearly neither Begala nor Carlson had a clue what Stewart wanted. They kept trying to figure out whether Stewart was asking them to be harder or easier on the people they interviewed. They seemed to think the only alternative to "beating up on someone" is "sucking up." Neither host had the first idea of what it might mean to be tough without being abusive.

Before you decide I'm putting a halo on Stewart, let me say that, ironically, Stewart didn't appear to grasp the difference either. Stewart called Carlson a "dick." I talk about the need to avoid labeling in later chapters. Perhaps different rules apply to a jester in Stewart's pay grade than ours. In any case, I invite you to practice what you preach when you make your appeals.

What was Stewart talking about, anyway?
While Begala and Carlson didn't understand what Jon Stewart objected to, the head of CNN President Jonathan Klein did. He said, "I guess I come down more firmly in the Jon Stewart camp." Klein went on to say he would prefer a substantive discussion of current events and controversies.

"I doubt that when the president sits down with his advisers they scream at him to bring him up to date on all of the issues," Klein said. "I don't know why we don't treat the audience with the same respect."

And I don't know why we don't treat each other with the same respect.

Note how Klein's comment contained some humor as well. The picture of the president's advisors screaming at him to keep him up to date is both illustrative and amusing.

The ball is in our court

Canceling *Crossfire* was a start. Jon Stewart's appeal got the conversation started. And no doubt, six-year's later, his "March for Reason" will add to the discussion. This book takes it from there. It will teach you what a reasonable dialogue is and how to have one. That way, you won't be following in the dubious footsteps of our national media.

Remember, this book is for *you*. So even if you don't care much for Jon Stewart, I invite you to make the Jon Stewart request at your kitchen table and water cooler. I don't suggest you say, "Stop being a dick."

You can say:

> *I'd love to have a collaborative discussion about (political issue.) However, as soon as the topic comes up, it seems things get adversarial. Let's have an honest conversation rather than a feud.*

And, in case you haven't noticed, I'm doing what Jon did. I'm asking you to:

A. **stop fighting,**
B. **stop parroting knee-jerk reactionary pundits who argue unrepresentative extreme positions**
C. **stop allowing emotional provocation to pass for dialogue**
D. **stop trying to win by overpowering,**
E. **and mainly to,**
F. **stop being part of politicians' divisive strategies**

I'm asking you to start being a part of a growing awakening group of people who Restore Sanity to Political Discussions.

I don't have Stewart's gift for humor, but I am a bit of a jester and a simpleton. I keep the tone light so my words can find their way past your defenses. I care very deeply, and sometimes the things I see and hear and the way we treat each other break my heart. It's a serious topic and the stakes are high. I want to say that on my planet, we don't behave that way. But on this planet, people do. And that's why I make my plea. That's why I invite you to make yours, graciously enough and clearly enough and collaboratively enough — and perhaps humorously enough — that others can hear.

Chapter 2

Big yeah buts and bigger yes ands

This book is for *you*. It would be an easier sell if I told you I was writing it for you to change others. I'm not, because I know your greatest resource is in your own responses. The delightful side-effect when you change is that others respond differently.

Okay, I hear some *big buts*. And some bigger *yes ands*.

Yeah, but #1...the other side is crazy, evil or both
It's always the other guy's fault, isn't it? And since this book is for you, how can it help when you're not the problem, they are?

Yes, and this is a dismissive and reductive attitude that will only shut conversation down. Yes, and it's more reason to talk. If they in fact are crazy, evil or both, why are those of us who care allowing them to have the floor?

While this book is for you, I'm not saying you're the problem and they get a pass. They might work very hard to win at your expense. People do twist the truth, manipulate, pressure and personally attack. People do speak to win based on tactics rather than communicate to collaborate.

And if you respond by being stunned into silence or agitated into aggression, you've lost, and so has our democracy. Blame them, and you're a victim. Learn how to respond, and you are empowered.

Let's repeat that:

> *Blame them and you're a victim. Learn how to respond and you are empowered.*

So if they seem crazy, evil or both, don't clam up. And don't say, "Stop being a dick."

You might say:

> *I'm interested in your ideas, but the way you're speaking feels aggressive and makes it hard to listen. Can we speak more graciously to each other?*

It might be the gentle shaking that will wake them up to what they're doing. Yes, and it might result in a little less insanity and evil in the world.

Yeah, but #2…it's impossible to know the truth.
It's hard to be graciously assertive when you're confused. And it's hard to not be confused when hundreds of voices scream at you daily. Actually, I'd be worried about you if you knew everything with complete certainty. I've been searching for deeper and deeper truths my whole life and continually uncover new layers.

If you listen to two different people describe what's going on in Iraq or Afghanistan, you'll think you're going crazy. The contrast is like you stepped into alternative universes on the Twilight Zone. It leaves you dazed and confused. Stunned into silence or agitated into belligerence. Guess what, that's the point, and that's why they call it "spin."

6

Yes, and you don't have to have all the answers to have an opinion. Yes, and you sure don't need to have all the answers to dialogue. Dialogue is about exchanging ideas to get closer to the truth, not asserting yours over someone else's. People who write and speak with complete certainty are suspect.

I'll give you a lot of tools to separate truth from propaganda in later chapters. Here, I just want to tell you to get comfortable with uncertainty. If you wait for absolute certainty, you'll never speak. Trust this: *manipulative political communicators are more than willing to fill the void whether they know what they're talking about or not.*

It's okay to say, "I could be wrong here, but I don't think so."

Yeah, but #3 ...it wont change anything anyway

Do you think it's hopeless? Is it too big? Are the cards stacked against you? Have you become cynical?

Yes, and despair is not an option. Cynicism is a coward's excuse. You overcome despair by taking action.

Remember, this book is for *you*. It's not your job to undo all the evils of the world. But how about some simple actions to become part of the solution instead of the problem?

For example, you could just hit *reply* instead of *send* when someone forwards an inflammatory email full of inaccuracies.

Say something like:

> *Hi, (name.) I received your email and want to let you know that it contains a large number of inaccuracies. I won't be forwarding it. Since accuracy in politics is important, please check the facts and send a correction to the list of people you forwarded this to. You can get more accurate information at (credible sources.)*

Feels good to take action, doesn't it?

Yeah, but #4...it's not MY problem
Do you think the nation's dysfunctional political dialogue is not your problem? Isn't that what some people are paid way too much money to do?

Yes, and you're in the car, aren't you?

Your family and friends are in the car, too, aren't they?

Shouldn't we at least try to leave this planet better than we found it?

Saying you don't care about politics is like saying you don't care about how you're allowed to live, what you're taxed on and how your taxes are spent. Here's an idea; Why don't you write a blank check and let someone else decide who gets to spend it?

You can't afford not to care. That's why I wrote this book for *you*.

Democracy isn't a spectator sport. While I don't suggest you say, "I'm through letting idiots like you silence me."

You can say something like:

> *Some people think it's rude to talk about politics. I think it's our responsibility as citizens. I'd like to exchange ideas.*

You may not have created the problem, and it's not up to you to single-handedly save the world. But it is up to all of us to be a part of the solution.

Yeah, but...#5 it's a mud fest
There's a saying, never wrestle with a pig. You both get all dirty and the pig loves it.

Yes, and that's why we need to clean it up. We can't let the mud-slingers, people who speak in doublespeak and who counter legitimate questions with personal assaults, tell us who we should hate and why. We can't let them drown out the people who ...make sense.

Yes, and don't wrestle with the pig. Don't play their muddy game. Learn how to change the game. Don't say:

> *I won't lower myself to your level.*

You could say:

This is too important to use personal attacks. I don't know if this kind of diatribe is fun for you, but I'd rather talk about how we can move forward than get stuck in the problems.

See how it works? The *yeah buts* are only an indication there is time for a *yes and*. It's an indication that we need to learn *How to Restore Sanity to Our Political Conversations*.

Chapter 3

From ~~Insanity~~ to Sanity — possible and necessary

Not-so-simple dialogue

- Taking *yeah buts* and turning them into *yes ands*.

- Taking problems and refocusing on solutions.

- Taking big problems and breaking them down into small action steps.

This is how we get the political dialogue jumpstarted. It's also how I've gotten hundreds of diverse groups talking to each other in my corporate training. This book is based on the tools and techniques, the experiences and the understandings I've garnered in 15 years as a communication author and a corporate trainer.

I facilitate difficult conversations. You know the ones. The conversations you dread, that you only begin by forcing yourself, and are relieved once they're over. The conversations that send the blood pumping to your major muscle groups in a fight-or-flight reflex, leaving no blood left for your brain. The conversations that come into perfect focus a day later when your heart stops racing and your brain gets its supply of blood back - and the ruminations of what you wished you had said haunt you relentlessly.

Those conversations. It's not just political conversations that can get us all riled.

But when I do my job right, these conversations are more engagingly therapeutic than traumatic. If I do my job right, they're more fruitful than frightening. If I do my job right, the conversation ends in a (metaphorical) group hug. If I do my job right, you'll be able to enjoy your political discussions too.

When all else fails, men turn to reason." ~ Abba Eban

Complements — not opposition

What you don't have in common you have in *complement*. I've seen it repeatedly in my difficult conversation facilitation: groups that appear to have nothing in common discover they have volumes in common, and what they don't have in common, they have in complement.

They discover how much they have in common or in complement when they stop judging and start considering.

They discover how much they have in complement when they stop assuming and start inquiring.

The Millennial and the Boomers go from adversaries to allies. The men and the women stop judging each other and start wanting to learn more. Managers and employees realize they're interdependent and stop blaming. Extraverts and introverts see what their counterparts add to the mix.

And if we handle our political conversations skillfully we end up embracing the person at the other side of the table whose ideas threatened us.

One conversation doesn't create perfect, everlasting harmony, but I've used it to bridge some pretty big divides.

My participants come to seminars with battle lines drawn, and end with that metaphorical group hug. If they can do it, so can divergent political adherents. Of course there are some external influences that add to the challenge.

Divide and profit

Sometimes work groups are adversarial because they're set up by systems that put them in competition with people they're supposed to be collaborating with.

In the political world, the issue is magnified. There are plenty of people who have a vested interest in keeping the spin going, keeping us agitated, and in feeding kitchen table hostility.

There is more profit and clout to be gained by many in power (big business, advocacy groups, politicos, etc.) by driving political wedges between us than there is by driving other kinds of wedges.

People stand to gain by deliberately driving a wedge between you and, say, your Uncle Joe. The ancient book *Art of War* is a popular political read that advocates the strategy of "divide and conquer." I don't have to guess; I know. Influential political operatives have read it and consciously apply the "divide and conquer" technique so they can "divide and profit."

Think about it. You don't see books on the shelves called: *Deliver Us from Evil: Defeating Terrorism, Despotism and **Women***. There's not a book called: *If **Extraverts** Had Any Brains, They'd Be **Introverts***. It probably wouldn't play well to release a book called: *How to Talk to a **Boomer**: If You Must*. And yet this kind of inflammatory title is the norm on the political shelf. Sure, some books do enhance the gender, generation and style divides, but not on the scale of the political divisiveness we see on the political shelves of our bookstores.

It's not a crazy conspiracy theory to suggest that external forces undermine the efforts of "We the People" to find a collective voice. But external forces aren't the point of *How to Restore Sanity to Our Political Conversations*. As much as I would love to get those who would divide us to STOP, that's beyond my scope - at least for now. I figure if Political Operative Lee Atwater's <u>repentance</u> didn't stop his colleagues from continuing in his divisive footsteps, and Dwight Eisenhower's admonition about the threat of the military industrial complex were ineffective, I expect my humble pleas would fall on deafer ears than theirs. There's too much in it for the big guys and gals to change. It's a bummer, I know.

> *"It took a deadly illness to put me eye to eye with that truth, but it is a truth that the country, caught up in its ruthless ambitions and moral decay, can learn on my dime." ~ Lee Atwater*

Those who would be divided

Here's the take-away. There are those who are intentionally divisive and there are those of us who allow ourselves to be divided. There's too much to lose to allow that division to continue. And we sure don't want to take it out on our families and associates.

I didn't write this for the would-be predators. I wrote this book for those of us who allow ourselves to be preyed upon.

This book isn't about how the left and right demonize each other in their political ads. It's about how you and I demonize each other's views at the dinner table.

It's about how the divide and conquer approach found its way into our homes, workplaces and relationships, and how we can restore sanity.

So you might say something like this:

> *You know, it's an election year and I notice things get inflamed and stirred up before elections. I respect your opinions and would like to be able to talk about the issues. Let's challenge ourselves to do it civilly, even though they're screaming at each other on the news.*

And we might also tell our candidate:

> *I just had the most stimulating conversation with someone who has a different stand than I do, about the issue of (issue.) We learned a lot from each other and didn't have to scream to be heard. I'd*

love to hear you have the same kind of substantive and authentic conversation on the topic.

"I view America like this, 70 to 80 percent are pretty reasonable people that truthfully, if they sat down on contentious issues could get along, and the other 20 percent of the country run it." ~ Jon Stewart

Laying the groundwork to restore sanity

So here's how I lay the groundwork to bridge the generational, gender and racial divides in my seminars:

1. Start with an agreed vision of the kind of dialogue we want. Everyone thinks they want to be reasonable before we touch the hot buttons. By agreeing about how we will talk to each other before we raise provocative issues, we open the channel for reasonable dialogue that is then easier to travel once we are triggered by contentious issues.
2. Set the stage for inquiry. I design interview questions for one demographic to ask about another demographic. By asking the questions, they get to know each other. It's humanizing.
3. Ask each group how they want to be treated.
4. Ask each group to translate complaints into requests.
5. Create a set of action steps for future dialogue.

In my seminars, step one takes about an hour, if I'm working with a group that has issues. In your conversations, it could be as simple as saying:

- *I bet if we tried, we could talk this through from the heart and not just get along while discussing this issue, but come up with some great new insights. I'd like that. Would you?*
- *How do you suggest we do that?*
- *I'd like to start with understanding a little about who you are and how it leads you to think the way you do. I'd like to share a little about me too.*
- *I'm find it difficult to listen when people (yell, don't let me speak, criticize me for my ideas, etc.) But I find when I feel respected, it's easy for me to listen to them.*

Here's how I don't lay the groundwork

I once attended a generational diversity seminar where the leader divided the group up by ages and had us list each generation with a plus (+) and (-) column.

We were instructed to list what we liked and didn't like about each group. It was amazing to see how the format brought out the judge, jury and executioner in each of the groups in a way a more considered approach did not.

It created a black and white scenario that lead to Reptilian Regressions.

Huh?

Read on.

Chapter 4

Political divisiveness is ingrained and inbrained

Triunication

Did you know you have three brains? (If you're thinking your political nemesis probably doesn't even have one, please read this book to the end before you open your mouth.)

I call the brain systems "brainlets."

It's called the Triune Brain System. Each brainlet processes information in its own way and if all goes according to plan, each brainlet communicates with the others to create a perspective that integrates the input of all three brainlets. I call that triunication. Personal triunication is when your heart, mind and will are in communication.

Interpersonal triunication is when two or more people speak with their hearts, minds and wills in synchrony.

When all doesn't go according to plan, the brainlets send conflicting messages that never get integrated and you have your own personal mental battlefield. The heart, mind and will are at odds. Open your mouth and you spread the lack of coherence.

You can be happily triunicating, when someone says something that takes you out. Suddenly you have what I call a Reptilian Regression, a Mammalian Meltdown, or Neocortical Apartheid.

Or I could also say your Izzie is triggered, your Webby is wounded and your Prof is sequestered. Yes, I will explain.

Humble, concrete beginnings

The first brainlet to develop in an infant is the sensory-motor brainlet, or the action brainlet. It's also called the reptilian brain(let), or in my language, Izzie.

So here's the deal. Infants exclusively develop the reptilian brainlet, or their Izzie, for the first year and a half of development. Izzie is responsible for the survival instinct. Izzie is concrete and physical, which is why babies explore their physical environments so enthusiastically. Izzie relates to the world through black and white, simplified concepts such as right and wrong, hungry and full, and can I eat it or will it eat me?

Can I eat it, or will it eat me?

I used contrasting words in the last sentence to engage your Izzie. Your Izzie was developed to guide your movements, and action requires contrast (e.g. you have to decide right or left before moving.) For Izzie, dichotomy is essential.

Your Izzie brainlet is your action, "ME brainlet."

Izzie is not a problem. But when Izzie usurps the thinking process, that's a problem. Which Izzie does, because Izzie is faster than his cellmates. That's what I call that a Reptilian Regression. When Izzie pulls you under and does all your thinking for you, the world becomes a dark and dangerous place that you need to defend against. You see enemies where there are none.

For example, if you call customer service when you're in a Reptilian Regression you'll alienate the very person who can help you. If you have a political conversation with someone you disagree with while you're in a Reptilian Regression, it's likely to do battle. Those who would divide us manipulate your Izzie if you don't know your Izzie better than they do. They say things like, *"(Group) wants to destroy life as you know it!"*

And if Izzie has an issue with that, all reason gets lost.

Now, let's look at your mammalian brainlet.

Lets get emotional
When a child becomes a toddler, the main developmental focus turns to the mammalian, emotional, limbic, relational brainlet. This brainlet is the We brainlet, so I affectionately refer to it as Webby. Webby starts with "We" and webs are all about connections, just as the emotional brainlet is.

The nickname "Webby" is cute and playful — and the mammalian brainlet likes cute and playful

We belong together!
Webby develops through play and relationships. The more developed your Webby is, the more refined your emotions become.

You can understand the difference between the reptilian and mammalian brainlets by looking at your pets. Your pet lizards don't have emotional brainlets, but your cat, dog and hamsters do. Your lizard has cold eyes, and your puppy has warm ones.

Your critters don't lose their reptilian brainlet capacity just because they also have mammalian brainlets. Their survival instincts are alive and well, which is the very reason they live to try to sleep on your bed another day.

By the way, when I make a personal comment, particularly one like referring to your pets, I stimulate your Webby. Most of us have a sweet spot in our hearts for some animal we have loved in our lives, and that sweet spot activates our Webby brain. I spent Thanksgiving this year with a couple whose faces lit up as they discussed their pet snakes. Even reptiles can evoke a Webby response.

Your pets' reptilian and mammalian brainlets talk to each other, each relating the type of information that is their specialty, and as a result, Fluffy and Fido make intelligent choices. Not intellectual choices, but intelligent ones, chosen in their own best interests. That's the definition of intelligence: the ability to act in accordance with your best interests. (If you think Fluffy and Fido are more intelligent than some policy-makers, you actually may be right.)

Can you see how political communication can manipulate your Webby? Associate their ideas with your sweet spot, and logic and action can go by the wayside.

Webby is an asset…until you hit a Mammalian Meltdown. That's when your emotions override your reflexive action and your logic. That's what goes on when someone who can't feed his kids spends thousand of dollars saving a pet that is way beyond saving, or when someone stays in an abusive relationship because the victimizer "really is a good person deep down." That's also what happens when we vote for a candidate that doesn't support our interests because he has a beautiful family.

A Mammalian Meltdown can lead to destructive choices because emotions overrule the vital input of your other brainlets. A Mammalian Meltdown also hinders reasonable political dialogue.

From me and we to it — now that's progress!
Let's move on to the early teens, when intellectual capacity develops. The WE brainlet and the ME brainlet are surrounded by developing IT brainlet. This is the faculty to stand back and observe with neutrality. It's not all about me any more. It's not all about us, either. It's impersonal, abstract and logical. It's your Neo-Cortical Brainlet. I thought about calling this brainlet IT, and I considered Spock, but settled on The Prof.

The Prof is your inner professor, your higher reasoning faculty and your technical capacity. The Prof interprets the information the other brainlets present to it, dissects it, reorders it, and applies meaning to it.

The Prof is the highest of the brainlets, but it's no less dangerous for the Prof to run the show than for Izzie or Webby. If the Prof is doing all your thinking for you, it's kind of like if a president tries to run a country without input from constituents.

It's fascinating to see how these weapons work

The Prof can look at the horrors of life without compassion and The Prof can examine threats without sensing danger. The Prof also can logically dismiss the concerns of those who experience compassion and sense danger.

Sometimes I watch commentators dissect events and wonder, have you no heart? Objectivity is good, but so is heart and will.

If The Prof operates in isolation, I call it a Neo-Cortical Apartheid.

We, Me or IT

Okay. So we have three brainlets and they each operate differently. Which one is best?

The answer is, none of them. If you operate from a single brain without guidance of the other two, you are being a "third-wit." You need all three brainlets, working together to navigate the great divides of life – including the great political divide. You need the action of the Izzie brainlet, the emotion of the Webby brainlet and the thought of The Prof brainlet. You need to integrate all three brainlets in order to restore sanity.

Izzie

I'm mad at someone about something, and someone will have to pay somehow. I'll show them who's boss.

Now, have you ever been so agitated that you were beside yourself? That's the Reptilian Regression. Chances are your reptilian brainlet was so triggered, it submerged you in its defenses and your mammalian brain and neo-cortical brain didn't stand a chance. I confess; I have had this happen to me on numerous occasions as the result of an inflammatory word or two spoken in a political discussion.

> *When dealing with people, remember you are not dealing with creatures of logic, but creatures of emotion.* ~*Dale Carnegie*

Webby
I just want us all to get along
Now, in case you didn't know, I'm a woman. Once a month my emotions play a stronger role in my life than other times. I sometimes experience a Mammalian Meltdown, where Webby dominates. Those aren't the best times for me to discuss emotionally charged political issues because my Webby gets her feelings hurt and takes everything so personally.

I see my Webby ability to feel as one of my best qualities. However, I have learned to guide those feelings with my Prof and Izzie abilities to reason and act effectively.

If you're crying over long-distance commercials, that's your Mammalian Meltdown hogging the show. Intellectually you know these people will get their phone service sorted out, but it seems so sad in the moment.

Yes, the plight of the victims of the world is tragic. Yes, and I would never want to stop caring and I don't want you to either. I do want to balance that caring with enough practicality that we can effectively navigate the waters of our political divides.

The Prof
Fascinating!
Some of us are intellectually dominant. My friend Kathleen responds to things I say with the words "interesting," and "fascinating."

When we're triggered, if our Profs take over, we don't have conversations, we present dissertations. If we have Neo-Cortical Apartheids, we might rationally explain that since there's no reason to be upset over something, we're not. Our Profs insist the issue is impersonal when our Izzie and Webby are screaming that it is very personal indeed.

We need all three perspectives in varying degrees. We need to triunicate.

If you're threatened by an intruder, you want your survival instincts functioning, but you do want logical and emotional input. When you're enjoying nature, you want your emotions flowing, but you don't want Izzie or The Prof to go to sleep. And when you're taking your SATs, you want The Prof to be sharp – but not to the exclusion of Izzie and Webby.

Me, We *and* IT: Triunication
Dale Carnegie and many in the sales world remind us that we are creatures of emotion, not creatures of logic. I say we are creatures of instinct, emotion and logic.

We need our Me and your We *and* our IT way of looking at the world. We need our action, emotion and thinking brainlets talking to each other. We need our wants, feelings and thoughts working congruently. We need our

Izzie, Webby and Prof to function together in order to deal effectively with life. We need personal triunication.

A United League of Brainlets lets us effectively discuss the things that matter — including politics. Our mental, emotional and volitional congruence lets us restore sanity and navigate the great political divide. Which I assume you want since you're reading this.

Those who would divide us

Those who seek to divide and conquer don't want unity. They know that by triggering a Reptilian Regression, a Mammalian Meltdown or a Neo-Cortical Apartheid, they can get us to react to the world around us in their best interests, not ours.

Some of those who seek to divide us do it consciously and knowingly. Others do it habitually. But this book isn't about them – it's about you and me and we who allow ourselves to be divided. It's time we stopped.

One way to keep from being taken out is to ask ourselves:
- What do I think?
- What do I feel?
- What do I want?

That engages all of our brainlets.

It helps us deflect divisive tactics when you understand how they work. That's why I'm spending so much time on inbrained political divisiveness. Let's look at some specific dynamics.

Meryl Runion

Chapter 5

Feeding fear and
Rousing Reptilian Regression

A scary national dialogue

If the questions a trainer asks at a seminar can create a Reptilian Regression within minutes, what do you suppose the questions our leaders ask us can do? Remember, the reptilian brain is the survival brain, and that means that once our survival is threatened, the Reptilian Regression tugs away. Can you think of any survival threats in our national lives and dialogues lately?

For my literal thinkers, I intended that last sentence as irony. The Prof tends to miss irony.

National events triggered our reptilian reactions, and many of our politicians and pundits reinforce our Reptilian Regression. That means many people in our lives walk around with their Izzies continually triggered or ready to be triggered.

Simply put, we're scared. I don't know anyone who isn't to some degree. We fear for our survival, and monitor the world for perceived threats to that survival. We live in a constant state of fear that activates our Izzies. We are faced with an enemy we don't see, so we turn to leaders to identify who the enemy is. That's something our leaders gladly do, with the help of pundits and ultimately our families, friends and neighbors. That isn't so simple, because who the enemy is depends on who you listen to.

There are plenty of people who sell their ideas, policies and themselves by identifying an enemy and promising to protect you from it. And there are plenty of people who sell ideas, policies and themselves by triggering your Izzie into a Reptilian Regression.

Three tips to upshift from the Reptilian Regression
Our security concerns aren't hysterical reactions to manufactured threats. We've heard it said that even paranoids have enemies. However, in order to navigate the political divide, you need to:

1. Resist the Reptilian Regression and upshift to look at things with all your faculties. (Personal triunication.)

2. Understand what causes Reptilian Regression so you can avoid triggering someone else's Izzie.

3. Master the language so your words lift your listeners out of their Reptilian Regression into full perception. (Their own personal triunication.)

Another way of saying this is you can navigate the great political divide by learning to integrate reason, emotion and instinct in your conversations, and inspiring others to as well.

Persuasion and manipulation
Marketers and propagandists speak directly to your Izzie. So do writers and good communicators. There's nothing inherently evil or unethical about speaking to Izzie. There is something unethical about deliberately flooding Izzie to create a reptilian reaction that is unmitigated by

compassion or reason. There is also something unethical about manipulating people to choose something that is decidedly against their own best interests.

Persuasion engages all three brainlets. Manipulation divides the brainlets. Persuasion considers the strengths of the three brains. Manipulation exploits the weaknesses of the brainlets. Manipulation brings out the worst in whatever brain it targets.

Let's look at persuasion and manipulation of Izzie.

Izzie traits and the tactics that exploit them

It's all about me
Our Izzies are self-involved. We all want to know what's in it for us, and it's appropriate that we do. Ideally, we temper our self-interest with compassion and logic to strike a balance. When out of balance, our greed becomes insatiable and is gratified without regard to others or to higher considerations.

It is ethical to send a message suggesting the listener take care of their legitimate self-interest. Unethical communication encourages Izzie to consider self-interest at the expense of others. Unethical communication masks, distorts or downplays the cost of policies to others.

Some say we have rampant consumerism because our Izzies are bombarded with messages that feed greed.
If you feel your greed manipulated, perhaps with promises of how you can get a bigger piece of the pie than you

deserve, you can say something like, "I'd like to have that, but since it would be unfair, I'm not interested."

I win

Izzie is competitive. Competition can be healthy and motivating. When unchecked it can be destructive and hostile.

It's appropriate to use the competitive nature to motivate toward a worthwhile end. It's inappropriate when competition is used to divide people who should be working cooperatively. I once conducted training in an office where the managers were pitted against each other so each week there was a winner and a loser no matter how well they all did. It was destructive.

Political conversations are often more about winning than understanding and exchanging ideas. If you feel the desire to win overtaking the conversation, you can say:

> *I'm interested in an honest, authentic dialogue. I'm not interested in competing to see who can trump the other.*

It's mine

Izzie is territorial. If we didn't defend territory against legitimate threats, we would not survive. If we become rigidly territorial, we create adversaries out of potential allies.

It is appropriate to appeal to Izzie's territorial nature when territory is legitimately threatened. It is inappropriate to appeal to Izzie's territorial nature to trigger fear and stimulate a Reptilian Regression.

If you notice territoriality taking over, you can say:
I'm feeling a defensiveness that seems reactive. 1 want to step back and see if this is a legitimate threat and respond rationally.

Me good, you bad

Izzie is judgmental. In order to survive, we must be able to evaluate our environments by applying sound judgment. When we are excessively judgmental, we close ourselves off from possibilities.

Gossip feeds Izzie's lust for judgment. It uses the flaws (or perceived flaws) of others as a way to foster allies at another's expense. It's called an unholy alliance.

The news has become gossipy lately, and as a result, issues fade into the background of discussion, turning politics into a personality contest.

Premature judgment undermines dialogue. It condemns without consideration.

If a political discussion seems gossipy rather than substantive, where a magnifying glass is focused on other's flaws to feed your Izzie's ego or the other person's ego, you can say, "I don't mind discussing candidates' suitability for their jobs, but this conversation feels kind of gossipy."

Petraeus Betrayus, Osama Obama

Izzie conflates ideas and believes the associations are real. Once Izzie has connected two concepts, it is difficult to separate them. For example, Kelly hated for the phone to ring when she worked in a corporation because it would inevitably be a problem she needed to solve. Now that Kelly has her own business, a ringing phone means money, but she still associates the sound of the phone ringing with a sense of dread.

Some communicators deliberately use concepts together to join ideas in Izzie's awareness. They may never say policy A promotes result B, but they will mention the two concepts in conjunction so Izzie will make the association. Political ads morph from the image of an opponent to visuals of terrorists. Voters may logically know there is no real connection, but feel an aversion to the disparaged candidate anyway.

If you hear someone making a conflated association (like saying a charismatic candidate is not to be trusted because Hitler was charismatic), you can say:

> *You know, I hear politicians deliberately create associations between ideas without ever quite stating that they're connected. That way they can plant these ideas in our brains without being accountable. I find it distasteful, and if we make associations I'd like for them to be clear, conscious and reasoned.*

Be afraid. Be very afraid

Izzie runs your fight or flight response. You must be able to respond immediately to legitimate threats. However, if you are stuck in fight or flight, Izzie is in reaction mode at all times. That decreases the likelihood of an appropriate response to a legitimate threat because there is little contrast between the legitimate threat and normal experience to get Izzie's attention. Plus, you'll burn out your adrenals, and miss the joy of life.

Media is well-known for selling fear. The motto of "if it bleeds, it leads" is alive and well.

Leaders know that a frightened populace is unlikely to question those who promise to protect them.

Intimidating communication tactics can undermine dialogue.

If someone feeds fear and that starts to trigger a fight or flight reaction, say, "Let's look at this logically."

They have a culture of death — We have a culture of life

Izzie likes contrast. I use contrast throughout this book. In the last paragraph, I contrast the value of an appropriate fight or flight response with the dangers of an inappropriate one.

Contrast is appropriate when the distinctions are real. It's inappropriate when they distort. Contrast is destructive when it oversimplifies and fixates on ways we differ to the exclusion of commonalities.

I find it useful to contrast personality styles in training, but I need to be careful not to imply the contrast is so great there is no meeting ground. Political show hosts often invite guests for extreme views rather than expertise because the contrast makes for lively debate, but results in a sense of unbridgeable division.

It's common for individual conversations to exaggerate contrast. If you think that's happening, you can say:

> *There's truth in what you say, but it's sounding black and white. I'd like to acknowledge more of the nuances.*

A three-step process to end our problems forever

Izzie likes simplicity. Izzie digests ideas in bite-size pieces. In this book, I continually refrain from unnecessary complexity. If I tell you everything I know, you'll learn nothing. If you try to share all your infinite wisdom with others, they'll miss your main points too.

Simplicity is appropriate when it doesn't degenerate into the simplistic. It is necessary to make a concept understandable, but it is destructive when simplification results in unrealistic assessment. (Suggesting you can cure a serious illness with a minor diet change would be simplistic.) Oversimplification can encourage people to ignore salient issues. Political ads are notorious for reducing complex policy questions to oversimplified summaries.

Because we've been led to believe the issues are simpler than they are, people who hold views that are more complex than the norm are often dismissed. If someone oversimplifies an issue, you can say:

> *I'd like it to be that simple. We're all looking for quick fixes. I've discovered over the years that it's just not that easy. I'd like to see a more detailed plan before I commit.*

Their hand is in your pocket

Izzie likes concreteness. Mental abstraction holds no appeal, which is why every abstract idea needs a concrete example to anchor it to the reptilian brainlet. When you describe a policy, you can anchor it to the reptilian brainlet by linking your ideas to your listeners' direct experience.

Examples are appropriate when they are truthful and representative. They are inappropriate when they are manufactured or unrelated. Izzie does not have the discernment to compare an abstract concept to a faulty example, and if your other brainlets aren't on the ball, you might overlook the discrepancy.

For example, if you're making a case that women aren't promoted as quickly as men in an organization, and you use a woman who lacks the skills for promotion to illustrate your point, it's a faulty example. If you're making a case for the idea that Joe is irresponsible with money and you use an example of when he was late with a car payment after his job was shipped overseas and his daughter required expensive surgery, it's a faulty example.

If you believe someone is using an example to anchor an idea that isn't appropriate, you can say:

> *Let's check our examples before we apply them. It could be a legitimate argument, but that example undermines its credibility because...*

Over and over and over and...over again

Izzie likes ritual and repetition. Shall I say that again? I will — just maybe not in the exact same words.

I've heard that radio advertising is ineffective unless you repeat the ads. Some suggest that if you don't plan to run a series of ads, you might as well not even bother.

Repetition is appropriate to reinforce a legitimate idea. However, as a well-known quote by Joseph Goebbels confirms, if you "repeat a lie often enough, people will believe it." That, of course, is exploitation.

If someone uses an oft repeated but unverified example, you can say:

> *It's tempting to believe that, because it's been repeated so many times. I'd like to check it out before I accept it.*

Mirror, mirror on the wall — you're better than those other schmucks

Izzie likes praise and attention. I continually recommend that managers make a point of acknowledging the things their employees do well. It's gratifying, effective, and if the manager means it, why not?

Authentic praise is different from insincere flattery, intended to pump Izzie up and leaving Izzie hungering for more. Legitimate praise is a gift, but flattery is a tactic which ultimately only serves the person who uses it.

Flattery is destructive when it divisively strokes the ego of one group by proclaiming their superiority over another. And, there's a dark side to the flattery. Anyone who pumps you up can tear you down as soon as you express an opinion they don't like.

If someone uses flattery, you can say:
> *Let's not make this about me. I don't need to be superior to anyone.*

> **"Flattery is no substitute for listening."**
> **~ Leland R. Beaumont**

Oh, the outrage of it all!
Izzie is susceptible to demonization, and can turn a misdemeanor into a felony. It is appropriate to encourage Izzie to protect self-interest. It is not appropriate when manipulators agitate Izzie into seeing an enemy around every corner, and into convicting others without the benefit of input from Webby and/or The Prof.

Politicians use feigned outrage on a daily basis. There are plenty of reasons for legitimate outrage, but the scandal-de-jour is often a distortion and magnification of something less valid. A great indicator of this is how differently politicians speak about a project, such as the building of a mosque, around election time than they do at other times.

If someone uses feigned outrage, you can say:

This is getting pretty dramatic, isn't it?

Get to know your Izzie
The more conscious you are of how you operate, the more immune you will be to manipulation. Get to know your Izzie better than marketers and political operators do. Pay attention to how your Izzie responds to messages that pull your strings. That way, you can be the one to pull your own strings. And you can hold your own in conversation that attempts to put you into a Reptilian Regression.

Chapter 6

They feel your pain (and sometimes exploit it)

Manipulating a Mammalian Meltdown
Webby dances to a different tune

Webby, or your relational brainlet, is like a completely different you, cohabitating in your brain with Izzie and Prof. The techniques and tactics that activate your Izzie don't have the same influence on Webby. But other ones do.

Marketers and political operatives understand how to activate Webby. The ethical ones inspire Webby to envision greatness. The ruthless exploit Webby into a manufactured Mammalian Meltdown. If you've ever gotten home with a product you wonder why you bought, it could be the effect of a skillfully manipulated Webby.

As a personal note, I am far more offended by tactics that manipulate my Webby than my Izzie. If I realize my greed was twisted into a false choice, I figure I got what I deserved. When my love and inspiration is exploited, I am far less benevolent in my assessment.

Ultimately, however, it all goes back to the fact that our greatest resource in any situation is or own response. Time spent whining about those who did us wrong is time not invested in creating the kind of world we want. No matter how outrageously people take advantage of our sensitivity, it is up to us to become aware of how our brainlets and political communication work. We have to use our WeQ realistically.

Let's look at what Webby responds to.

We, us, belong, join, connect

Webby is a joiner. Webby likes to feel connected. Words that imply that we're in this together appeal to Webby. I use the word "we" throughout this book to talk to your Webby, and I make comments here and there to let you know that I've experienced the same kinds of things you have. And, in fact, I have. When I say we're in this together, I'm not just working your Webby. I'm letting your Webby know we have shared experiences.

It's effective to identify the common ground we share in order to appeal to Webby. It's manipulative to feign common ground. Many politicians pretend they are "just plain common folks" when they come from a very different elite background.

When someone talks like an elite leader is a regular guy (or gal), you can say:

> *Many politicians come across like they're just like us, but if you look at their history and their life choices, it's clear they're not. That doesn't mean they can't be good politician, but I don't want to select someone because they're like me when they're not.*

An ostracized Webby can get desperate

Webby doesn't like being excluded. People sometimes present things as more popular than they are — or more on the fringe — in order to encourage Webby to belong to the "in crowd" and reject those who are "out of the mainstream."

People have done desperate things to belong. Like stay silent and go along to get along with people who manipulate Webby. Like pretending not to hold an attitude because people who hold those attitudes are subject to ridicule. Some of our Webbies never graduated from our high school emotional life. They're still playing the game invented by a select few to avoid being ostracized, rejected, isolated and otherwise shunned from the tribe.

If someone tries to change your mind based on popularity, you can say:

> *If (candidate) is out of the mainstream, maybe I am too. That's okay. I like her policies and don't need anyone else to agree to support her.*

Pack the bags — Webby takes a victim/guilt trip

How dare you even suggest…? You fill in the blanks. Some Webbys are silenced by the suggestion that beliefs and ideas are shameful, disloyal or hurtful. Webby brings a different kind of intelligence to the conversation. She doesn't operate with linear IQ, she operates with what author Jeffrey Armstrong calls WeQ.

It is appropriate to appeal to Webby's caring conscience. We can all lose our connection to our sense of community at times. If someone deliberately triggers shame, it's manipulation.

If you feel tinges of guilt or shame, check in to see if your Webby is being manipulated. You can say:

> *My heart is clear on this one. I don't enjoy sharing an opinion that you find distasteful, but I know this is how I see it.*

Webby likes to play. Add a little fun to a seminar and my group's learning quotient goes way up. I've been playing with you since the first words of this book. Why? Because I take the subject seriously, and I want what I say to get in. Okay, I've also been doing it because I like to have fun too. When you have your political dialogues, add levity by adding fun — good clean fun at no one's expense.

The fun factor is seriously exploited by entertainment news, which clutters the airwaves and makes it more difficult for genuine issues to emerge. We could end up entertaining ourselves down the proverbial primrose path. But a bit of play and levity can make your opinions palatable.

If the entertainment value seems to usurp substance, you can say:

> *This is fun, and I don't want to be a buzz-kill, but I don't want to forget that this is a decision that affects our lives.*

You make my heart sing

Webby responds to music. If you add music to your message, it draws Webby into the discussion. If you can't use actual music, use word music. I slip alliteration, rhythm and rhyme into my writing every chance I get. It's not quite a jingle, but Webby likes it.

Can music be manipulative? Yes — when it is used to evoke emotion to override rather than complement Izzie and The Prof. If music creates a dramatic moment that conflicts with what you think matters, address it. Otherwise the music will linger unconsciously and color the reality. You can say:

> *That music was deeply moving. However, with what I know about the situation, I think a better score would have been (name).*

Webby is the home of imagination. Describe your vision of possibilities, and Webby is all ears. I have a video called *A World of Truth* that opens with the words, "Imagine a world where everyone says what they mean and means what they say without being mean when they say it." Izzie loves the repetition and contrast; Webby loves the vision. The entire movie details my vision for such a world.

Advertising exploits the visionary imagination by marketing consumerist visions of *having*. Politicians sometimes (okay, often) substitute empty catch phrases for genuine visions.

If you communicate your sincere vision of what is possible, it will motivate others. Or at the very least, it will motivate you. Writing my vision in this book is one of the most inspiring things I've done in a very long time.

If someone creates a vision that does not seem to have a basis in reality, say so. You can say:

> *You paint a tempting picture. It will take a lot of concrete detail for me to believe it could be real, however.*

Join us...

Webby likes to belong. Reassure Webby that there are plenty of others taking the stand you're promoting, and most Webbys will want in. Blogs are popular in part because they let people belong to a group.

Advertisers exploit Webby when they suggest you'll be "left out" if you don't buy or otherwise do what they want you to. Many politicians frame opinion they want to discredit as held by fringe groups, which means if you hold that opinion, you don't belong to the "in-group." (Often the polls discredit "fringe-group" labels. Other times the issues the groups stand for are popular, but the public rejects the group itself due to chronic misrepresentation and ridicule.)

Express your ideas like invitations. Jon Stewart did that when he invited Begala and Carlson to "join us."

Webby loves family, community and country. Start talking about yours and your listener will be thinking about theirs. For many people, having kids was one of the biggest things they ever did in their lives. That's why it can create an instant connection when you mention yours.

No political speech is complete without at least four comments about family and five flags in the background. Sometimes the politicians who flaunt family have disregarded their own. And if patriotism is highlighted by someone who willingly sells out the country's interest for personal profit, it's manipulative.

That said, don't bypass this power of legitimate references to the heart string tweakers. If you are concerned about a policy because you want a better future for your kids, say so. Say:

> *I have four kids and I want to leave the world better than I found it for them.*

Webby watch

Watch your Webby respond to the world around it. See what evokes your Webby and pay attention to your Mammalian Meltdowns, especially when you suspect manipulation is behind your meltdown.

Communicate by using but not abusing Webby.

Meryl Runion

Chapter 7

Rationalize = rational-lies
(and other neo-cortical cons)

Ivory tower truths have consequences
If there's one brainlet I know, it's the neo-cortex. I spent most of my life living there. I grew up in an academic family. My parents are/were very smart people. I was pretty smart myself, and very lacking in intelligence.

When I think of some of the things I did in my twenties, I cringe. If you knew me then and were chilled by my cool logic, please accept my apologies. It made sense at the time...

Making sense is only part of the story. Lies can seem very rational. That's why it's called rationalize / rational lies. My Neo-Cortical Apartheid was so severe that I passed on graduate school so I could get down from my ivory tower. I had to reclaim my heart, and my instincts.

Sometimes pundits, political operatives and politicians conduct cool, rational discussions about topics that would tear at the heartstrings of anyone whose heart was open and would set alarm bells off for those whose instincts were awake. And yet the conversation continues as if there were no human consequences to the issues discussed.

While many political shows target Izzie and to some extent Webby, National Public Radio generally addresses The Prof and Webby. (Am I the only one who wonders if NPR would report the destruction of an entire continent with the same calm dispassion they use when they talk about restaurant tips? I hope we never find out.)

A Neo-Cortical Apartheid may seem safer than experiencing life directly, but it isn't.

Here's more about how The Prof experiences life when left to his own devices.

It's an impersonal world out there

Izzie is your Me brainlet and Webby is your We brainlet. The Prof brainlet is the IT brainlet. The Prof embraces pure logic without the "messiness" of emotion or instinct. To The Prof, everything is objective and impersonal. The Prof is objective in the true sense. Life is an object to be analyzed, evaluated and logically ordered. The Prof relates to analysis without the personal touch. The Prof likes to know that A+B=C. How you feel about it is a distraction.

Without the guidance of the instinctive and emotional brain, The Prof can seem — and be — coldly impersonal, and even cruel. Cold logic can argue for the unconscionable, as if there was no human impact.

That makes sense

Logical arguments are music to The Prof. The Prof loves to take the seemingly random and uncover the inherent order in it. Organize your points in logical order, and emphasize the order you use, and your listener's Prof will respect you in the morning.

Less sophisticated or lazy Profs can be misled by arguments that sound logical but aren't. All they need to hear is Prof language and they're satisfied.

I describe several logical fallacies in chapter 22. There exist an unlimited number of fallacies. But by studying the ones I detail, you'll be more aware of logic that isn't logical.

Is it possible?

The Prof doesn't ask if it's appropriate to do something, only if it is possible. Intellectual challenge is The Prof's domain – morality and ethical considerations are outside the domain. There are many examples of inhumane research projects during WWII. Well, I'm not sure we need go back that far at all.

If someone seems unaware of the human implications of policies and decisions, they might be stuck in a Neo-Cortical Apartheid. Don't let them trigger one in you, where you forget that people aren't just bugs in a jar. Remind yourself and others of their families and other aspects of their human natures. And notice when your conversation becomes about what's possible without considering human factors.

You can say:

> *This discussion sounds very logical and reasonable. But it seems to me we don't have the level of compassion we need to be exploring these things.*

51

Complexifying

I once read a Political Science article called "How to Make a Simple Truth Complex." It hit close to home. I had learned the art of writing complex sounding papers that got me A's. My Prof used big words and complicated explanations rather than the simpler concepts that got me B's at best.

When my son worked a computer help desk, he occasionally would turn his Prof up and talk over the customer's head to get the customer to stop acting like they knew everything and listen. It worked, but it was a kind of manipulation.

If someone makes a complex argument that goes over your head, it could be a complex situation, or it could be that instead of simplifying, they're "complexifying." Okay, complicating. "Complexifying" complexified my point. They could see the world through a Neo-Cortical lens, or they might be banking on your unwillingness to appear stupid.

If someone is overcomplicating a topic, don't hesitate to ask for a simpler explanation. You can say:

- *I'd like to hear that explained in layman's terms.*
- *Pretend I'm five years old and explain it to me.*
- *Can you explain that with examples I can relate to?*

Definitely avoid being intimidated by their big, erudite words.

Exacting trumps practicality

Intellectual purists can drive you crazy. Their Profs become obsessed over minor inaccuracies that really don't matter. For example, in researching logical fallacies, I discovered that the fallacy called "begging the question" has changed meaning over the years. The internet is full of hostile arguments among intellectuals about what it really means. Sure, accuracy is important, but there comes a point where it makes more sense to call it good enough and move on. In the hours these people spent trying to convince each other what "begging the question" really means and how it should be used, they could be snuggling with their sweethearts — if they have them.

This type of exacting can be narrowness, but it also can be a form of dominance or avoidance that distract from important issues. You can say:

> *I love precision too. But there comes a time when we need give up our intellectual perfectionism and move on. Your arguments are interesting, but this conversation is feeling unbalanced to me now.*

Reduction

The Prof narrows reality to what it has language for. Orwell knew that, which is why his book *1984* described a ministry of words that destroyed words that described concepts Big Brother didn't approve of. Winston realized, "It is not just language that is being destroyed, the attempt is to annihilate consciousness and thought itself. Once newspeak has taken over completely, thought crimes will be impossible, because there will be no language to express rebellious thoughts in."

Whoa!

The Prof categorizes and names the world and thinks it knows it. If he doesn't have a word for something, it's as if it doesn't exist.

And if he does, he can reduce the nuances and multi-dimensional nature of life, love and politics to labels and facts and figures.

If you feel yourself the victim of reductionism that puts you or an argument into a category and stops at that, you can say:

- *That's one aspect of the situation. But it's much more than that.*
- *Labels stop thought.*

Removed

To the Prof, God is a dictionary definition. The intellect prefers a lecture on heaven to heaven itself.

Interrogation techniques are reduced to classifications regarding torture or non-torture. Patients are reduced to their symptoms or diagnosis. A flower is experienced by its name and function. The term Ivory Tower came about for a reason. It is both removed and chillingly cold.

If a comment or argument seems removed, you can say:

What do you feel about that?

Tunnel vision

The Prof isolates to analyze. He regards his subject as existing separately from the environment. Medical doctors are often criticized for isolating diseases and not regarding the disease in context. In fact, some suggest that their focus on disease omits the broader context of health.

Wendy experienced this tunnel vision when she presented a proposal to her faculty and all comments were regarding minor technical errors. She backed the group up and asked, "Hey, can we look at the big picture? Am I on the right track? Is this what you are generally looking for?" It was, but it hadn't occurred to anyone to tell her that. They all became narrowly focused on the minor errors.

When you experience tunnel vision you can do what Wendy did and say:

Hey, can we look at the big picture here?

The best and the worst of the brainlets

The Neo-Cortex is the highest of the Triune Brain system, and yet it is in many ways the most dangerous when left to its own devices. The Prof has all of the intellect and none of the street-smarts of the earlier brainlets. He has capacity without heart or instinct. That's why it's important to say "no" to a Neo-Cortical Apartheid, and "yes" to a League of United Brainlets and use our minds in the way they were designed. It's important that we triunicate.

Chapter 8

Words that stroke, evoke, cloak and provoke

Target your words
One of my SpeakStrong catch-phrases is: "Speak as if every word matters. It does." It's true. But every word matters in a different way to each of your brainlets.

Here's where all the brainlet information gets really practical. Since each of the brainlets have their radars tuned to different information, different words stimulate each one. Izzie words are survival/action words, Webby words are feeling/visioning words, and Prof words are intellectual words.

When you read the lists below, keep in mind that we all react to words differently according to our personal associations. Also keep in mind that the words will have different impact in different contexts. Please do not regard the lists below as either absolute or complete. (Sorry Izzie — I know you like things simple.)

Caring + reason + strategy = Bulls eye

I divide words into lists of aversion words and attractor words for both Izzie and Webby. I found the aversion words much easier to find than attractor ones. Interesting, huh!

I start with Izzie words. The words on the first Izzie list tend to activate fear and can trigger fight-or-flight. The words on the second Izzie list address what your Izzie wants: security. While you read through these lists, notice how they affect you.

Izzie aversion words:
Endanger, should, wrong, betray, mushroom cloud, collapse, crisis, enemy, n----, insecure, threaten, criticism, audit, loser, urgent, impose, traitor, fascist, B---, terrorist, coerce, corrupt, decay, destroy, devour, endanger, failure, greed, lie, pathetic, whiner, overthrow, radical, shallow, sick, waste, crumble, expose, hazard, blight, ruin, weaken, mercenary, rotten, enemy, criminal, weak, debacle, exploit, evil, vicious, inhuman.

Examples: "I have some criticism for your book." "Why would you endanger me that way?" "You're destroying our relationship." "We don't want this project to result in failure."

Izzie attractor words:
Provide, protect, reliable, control, tough, security, dependable, you're right, preserve, want, property, mastery, build, crusade, work, reward, strength, might, dominance, save, defend, strengthen, fortify, guarantee, win, triumph, prevail, victory, conquest, stable, permanent, steadfast, strong, powerful, lasting, unwavering, sturdy, tenacious, determined, constant.

Examples: "We need to show our strength at the meeting." "This will preserve our equity." "We must maintain global dominance."

All too familiar

How are you feeling about now? Any signs of a Reptilian Regression?

You'll recognize many of the words on both lists. You hear them on the news and in political ads daily.

I shared many of these words in one of my training sessions and asked the group what they thought of the list. The response was "It sounds familiar."

Of course these words have legitimate uses. If someone is corrupt, it's appropriate to call them that. The misuse comes in when these words are used — as they often are — to create a Reptilian Regression that obstructs logical assessment of their appropriateness.

Webby words:

There's a completely different set of words that engage your Webby brain. The words on the first Webby list activate emotional disdain in the Webby brain, and the words on the second list address what Webby wants.

Webby aversion words:

Insensitive, dread, shallow, disgust, isolation, alone, hate, greed, pathetic, hypocrite, selfish, radical, challenged, unfair, shame, unpatriotic, angry, guilt, humiliating, stain, fringe, disgrace, slander, godless, defile, stigma, disrespect, ridiculous, bizarre, moron, ludicrous, freaks, absurd, nutty, loons, weird, extremist, out-of-the-mainstream, wavering, immoral, evil, unethical.

Examples: "If you don't vote yes, you'll be isolated." "It's ludicrous to think he broke the law." "This idea is a disgrace."

Are you depressed yet? If so, read on to the Webby attractor words. They are the antidote.

Webby attractor words:
Mom, children, love, inspire, vision, imagine, ideal, we, heart, hope, community, feel, inspire, precious, fair, vision, connect, relate, comfort, home, neighborhood, create, stimulate, motivate, share, cooperate, team, melody, harmony, unite, agree, hearten, encourage, family, nourish, proud, brave, courageous, help, confident, dream, empower, humane, learn, truth, moral, love, together, integrity.

Examples: "Let's pull our community together to promote our vision."

Words that win the Prof's attention and respect
When we get to The Prof words, an interesting thing happens. There is only one list. Because The Prof is neutral, there aren't the dual words you saw in the Izzie and Webby lists.

Here's a list to give you an idea of what words get The Prof in gear. Notice how they affect you.

Think, reason, theory, probability, mind, reflect, calculate, conjecture, empirical, consider, principle, equation, first...second...third..., practical, method, premise, system, postulate, rationale, proposal, thesis, sequential, surmise, deduce, hypothesis, analysis, data, abstracts, inference, surmise,

Example: "The probability of success is minimal." "Recent news reports provide rationale for sequential withdrawal."

These words are by no means exclusive, but by now you should be aware of the general affect words have on your brain.

Tune your radar to the impact of words
Choose your own words with care, understanding the power they have to activate brainlet activity. Observe how others use these words so you can see how they influence your own perceptions.

Master propagandists know what they're doing when they heap the avoidance words on those they wish to diminish and apply the attractive words to themselves. If these words sound familiar, it's because they are.

You and the people on the other side of the great political divide have been bombarded with powerful words for a very long time. Learn how these powerful words work so you can choose to respond. Recognize the Reptilian Regression, Mammalian Meltdown and Neo-Cortical Apartheid so you won't be caught in their spell.

Then, learn how to triunicate so your words will embody heart, mind and will.

Chapter 9

The courage of conviction

Know why you care

Why do you care enough to try to bridge the great political divide? That's a serious question that I want you to find a sincere answer to.

One of my readers wrote to ask me how he could talk to his daughter about the story behind the story in the news. She shut him down at every turn. I shared much of the information you're reading in this book with him. But to be able to answer him specifically, I'd need to know why it was important to him to be able to talk with his daughter about these things.

My ultimate guideline for communication in all things is to: "say what you mean and mean what you say without being mean when you say it." To say what you mean, you need to *know* what you mean. What do you think, what do you feel and what do you want?

Know what having an open, informative, civil, productive dialogue would mean to you. Know *why* you care so you can *communicate* why you care. What is the source of your passion? If you're only mildly interested, you won't have the courage of conviction to keep going if the person you want to dialogue with becomes combative or dismissive.

The word "courage" has its basis in the French word Coeur, which means "heart." How cool is that?

You won't have the will to pull yourself out of it if their resistance triggers a Reptilian Regression, Mammalian Meltdown or a Neo-Cortical Apartheid in you. We're talking about taking on the big one here, and you're unlikely to do what it takes to take on the big one with mild concern.

Why *I* care: the source of my passion
Make a list of the reasons why you care. Here's mine to jumpstart you.

I care about reasonable political dialogue for many reasons, including:

- I care about reasonable political dialogue because without it we operate in the dark and govern in the dark. That's as dangerous as driving in the dark without headlights. I have nightmares about driving in the dark but I can wake up from those nightmares. I can't wake up from the political dialogue nightmare. It's a waking nightmare, and I'm afraid we're going to crash.
- I care about reasonable political dialogue because I've lived through the nightmare of having serious legitimate concerns dismissed. I couldn't find anyone willing to discuss them or do anything about the situation. My concerns proved legitimate, we crashed and it was horrific.
- I care about reasonable political dialogue because emotionally I like connecting and I dislike barriers. Any off-limit topic feels like a wall that separates me from others.

- I care about reasonable political dialogue because the contemptuous debate and diatribe that substitute for it are an assault on my sensitivities. It pains me. It hurts my heart, even when I agree with the conclusions of the propagator.
- I care about reasonable political dialogue because I care about the future of the United States. I believe in the principles our country was founded on. I'm a mom, and I want my son to grow up in a nation based on those principles. I feel a responsibility to all children to pass the world on in better shape than I found it. How can that happen if we can't talk reasonably about issues?
- I care about reasonable political dialogue because I care about open communication in general. Dysfunctional, polarizing, contentious political discussions set the tone for dysfunctional, polarizing, contentious discourse among individuals. The personal contention hurts my heart even more than the national contention.
- I care about reasonable political dialogue because I love the pursuit of truth and justice. Illogic passing as reason confuses me.
- I care about reasonable political dialogue because it makes sense to have it.

That's my list. I started with my Izzie reasons, moved to Webby reasons and concluded with the Prof. That's a format you can use to make your list too.

The high price of silence
Have you ever stayed silent when something needed to be said...and regretted it? I have, and the current political

conversation climate feels like "deja-vu all over again." The first time I let myself be silenced, I paid an enormous price.

It happened in 1986. I tell the story in my book *PowerPhrases!* and also in *How to Use PowerPhrases.* Here's a quick summary:

My first husband became ill in 1986 and shut down my concerns that it might be serious. I allowed him to silence me and tried not to rock the boat. Nine months after I told him I suspected he had cancer and he would not let me talk about it, he died of untreated cancer. Being right offered no solace. (As an FYI, I'm remarried and life is good.)

It's possible that if I had continued to speak despite the pressure on me not to, my late husband would still be with me today. I review the experience, not to self-flagellate, but to remind myself why silence is not an option for me now.

The national conversation feels very much like my former marital conversation did during my husband's illness. Here are similarities between my silence then and the national conversation now:
- I had a sense something was very wrong and no one was talking about it.
- I had ideas of what the problems were.
- I was discounted and treated like a troublemaker when I tried to talk about it.
- There was cognitive-dissonance. What I perceived as happening and what I was told was happening didn't match.

- Reasons people used to discount my concerns did not make sense to me.
- My observations were confirmed over time.
- There was a lot at stake.

I felt an urgent need for reasonable dialogue and action with my late husband in 1986, and I feel an urgent need for dialogue and action in our nation now. If I'm right this time like I was last time, I will take no joy in saying "I told you so."

Forget guarantees

If I had Spoken Strong in 1986, my husband might still be with me today. Or he might not. There are no guarantees. Except for one guarantee: if enough of us stay silent because there are no guarantees, we'll never find our common dreams and we'll never get a voice. Reading political blogs, I'm often dismayed by nay-sayer comments that attempt to silence those who suggest signs of progress, hope for improvement or ways to get individual voices heard. The nay-sayers and "ain't it awfullers" drown out the reasoned exploration of possibilities with attacks on the person who dared to suggest some cause for hope or positive action.

Speaking Strong is not about guarantees. It's about standing up for what you believe. It's about sharing what you know. And it is about exploring ideas through open, reasoned dialogue.

It's also about maintaining your own integrity regardless of outcome. Several years after I lost my husband to cancer, my best friend started showing cancer symptoms. I expressed my concerns clearly, directly and kindly. My friend ignored my concerns and her doctor's advice and I lost her too. But I didn't lose myself.

If you speak up and no one covers your back, at least you were honest. And who knows, you just might start something.

Dialogue, not diatribe
Many assume if they're not attacking, they're acquiescing. Many assume if they're not dominant, they're dominated. Many assume if they're not aggressive, they're complicit. I'm sure there are many people who did not get this far in this book because they assume that the alternative to arguing is acquiescing.

I'm talking about doing what works and being CLEAR.

There's a difference between having a big mouth and having a mighty one.

You know there's a Mighty Mouth in every one of us and it's really not that hard. You just say what you mean, and you mean what you say. Just be sure you're not mean when you say it.

So go for a learning dialogue, not an overpowering diatribe. They're far more likely to hear what you say.

Get convicted
Your reasons for caring will be different than mine. Figure out why you care, and talk about it. People will care more about what you know when they know why you care. They

need to know what your words mean to you. And if you know that, it will give you the courage of conviction.

You can say:

I'm passionate about this because...

Chapter 10

*Differences between conservatives and liberals
(real ones — not the Madison Avenue versions)*

Stepping into the fire

When you read the chapter title, did you automatically assume I'm going to tell you how vastly superior one political leaning is to the other? After all, the national political discourse makes liberals and conservatives out to be natural enemies.

I am human, and that means I have my own point of view. Despite my efforts and the efforts of my reviewers to maintain neutrality, there may be some imbalance here. And as a fellow human too, you might see some judgment in these pages that isn't really there. Let me know how well I succeed at neutrally describing the difference between the political opposites. And please be gentle when you do.

To me, claiming one political leaning to be superior to the other is as illogical as suggesting men are better than women or vice versa. It makes as little sense as suggesting dogs are better than cats, or detail people are better than creatives.

While one group can claim superiority over the other in some situations and for some things, no group can claim it overall.

Liberals and conservatives operate differently, and they tend toward different strengths and weaknesses. A trait that's adaptive in one setting could be maladaptive in another.

Quick, think of your "political opposite." Can you think of ways you could benefit from being more like them and the group they lean toward politically? If you're honest, I'm sure you can.

That's why we need each other, in much the same way the three brainlets need each other to operate functionally.

Not just a political landmine
There are inherent dangers in defining traits, tendencies and characteristics of demographic and psychographic groups in any kind of diversity discussion. The same dangers exist and are magnified in a diversity discussion. The divisiveness of the political landscape is so intense that any description is likely to be assumed to be biased. The slightest mention of a strength or weakness associated with one side or another will incite some readers to dismiss everything else I say.

Is neutrality possible? Yes. Whether it's easy or not is another question, but possible? Yes. My being female doesn't prevent me from describing how men and women are different (beyond the obvious) in my corporate training. (Interestingly, the men tend to agree with my descriptions of them more than the women do.)

If I can define common traits of the genders, generations and styles, and be perceived as acceptably balanced, maybe there's hope I can define the main differences between conservatives and liberals as well. And maybe you can too.

Predefinition disclaimers
Before you consider conservative/liberal qualities, review the following guidelines and warnings to keep the discussion a unifying one rather than a divisive one.

A. Use the information for understanding and relating rather than reinforcing stereotypes
Any tool or skill can be abused. Use this information to perceive the uniqueness of each individual, to draw on the strengths you perceive, and to navigate and resolve the great divide. Don't use it to superimpose stereotypes over your direct experience.

B. Consider the descriptors as tendencies rather than absolutes
Avoid Izzie's black and white thinking. For example, don't assume someone who values autonomy is so anti-authority that they'll resist anything authority figures do. Use these ideas as indicators, not labels. Paint with a thin brush, not a broad one.

C. Consider conservative / liberal as one scale among many
There are thousands of ways we could classify people; to put them into one of two categories is limiting. Yet we classify people as liberals or conservatives daily. Since the categories are so prevalent, I address it here to add clarity to the prevailing definitions.

While you read these definitions, remember — few people fit neatly into a liberal OR conservative definition, and these descriptions only paint partial pictures.

D. Regard the descriptions as continuums rather than two distinct categories

Political differences run on a continuum. A moderate liberal could easily have more in common with a moderate conservative than with an extreme liberal (and vice versa.) Consider these descriptions as continuums with the prototypes only defining the two poles.

E. Recognize that every quality has a strength and a limitation depending on situation and degree

Be aware that the traits on either side of each continuum below are positive in the right situation in the right intensity, and can be destructive in other situations and when unchecked.

Differences defined

Okay. Hold your breath, plug your nose and let's dive in. With these guidelines in mind, here are some of the traits that research and social commentators and my own observations attribute to the different sides of the political spectrum:

1. Autonomy / Authority

Liberals / Autonomy

Liberals value individual autonomy and individual decision-making. They like to leave decisions to individual judgment and conscience whenever possible, and for consensus when necessary. Many suggest the Democratic Party is a loose coalition rather than a political party. It takes a while to reach consensus, because everyone has input.

It is generally stressful for liberals not to be able to make their own decisions.

> **Autonomy upside:** Being autonomy-based leads to creativity. Autonomy-based individuals can act with a minimum of supervision. Autonomy-based decisions elicit buy-in by other autonomy-based individuals.

> **Autonomy downside:** Being autonomy-based can also result in inaction, chaos and reinvented wheels. Autonomy-based individuals can be uncooperative on teams. The common comparison is "it's like herding cats."

> **Autonomy example:** Tom Brokaw talked about how Democratic White Houses have many factions. One administration official contradicts another — which makes for lively news stories. Democrats tend to speak in many voices.

Conservatives / Authority:
Conservatives value authority and centralized decision-making. They like guidelines clearly defined. They favor a top-down hierarchy of power and authority, and generally do not question decisions that are handed down.

Authority upside: Being authority-based can be highly efficient because all members work together in lockstep. Authority-based teams function efficiently.

Authority downside: Being authority-based can stifle creativity and lead to overlooking on-the-ground realities and opportunities. It can lead to mistakes and bad policy unchecked.

Authority example: Tom Brokaw reported that in Republican administrations, every representative says exactly the same thing. Many Republicans pride themselves on being "on message."

2. Adaptable / Stability

Liberals / Adaptability

Liberals are open to input and therefore are likely to adjust and realign accordingly. They tend to like flexibility and fluidity in their environments.

Adaptability upside: Adaptability is useful to adjust to a changing world. What worked yesterday might not work today. The adaptable among us are early adopters and quick to incorporate new opportunities when they arise.

Adaptability downside: Early-adopters and early-adapters sometimes abandon the tried and true for a less useful novelty. They can fail to build structure in favor of the "flavor of the month." This adaptability can create an instability that lacks foundation. Liberals are often labeled "flip-floppers," and whether the label is applied appropriately or not, it can stick because when the liberal tendency of adaptability is not balanced by a stable foundation, it creates chaos.

Adaptable example: Liberals adopted internet technology more quickly than their conservative counterparts.

Conservatives / Stability

Conservatives value the consistency of the tried and true. They set their direction and stay with it.

Stability upside: This consistency builds a foundation for security and stability. It can produce the kind of results that take time to build.

Stability downside: If individuals and cultures are unable to adapt to change, the entire structure can crumble.

Stability example: Conservatives built an infrastructure to support their objectives piece-by-piece over many years. Rather than just focusing on the next election, they spent many years developing foundations, think tanks, endowed professorships, media outlets and other aspects of a political infrastructure that is not matched on the liberal side.

3. Individualistic / Societal norms

Liberals / Individualist
Liberals are individualistic. They like time alone and see themselves as individuals first, and part of a larger group second. They'll say, "I gotta be me."

> **Individualist upside:** Society consists of individuals. When individuals develop their individual strengths and characteristics rather than trying to conform to the qualities societal norms reinforce, they tend to be happier. That can benefit society.

> **Individualist downside:** Society consists of individuals. When individuals develop without regard for the greater needs of society, it can detract from the greater good. Individualism to an extreme is narcissistic.

> When there are no agreed-upon standards of behavior, people don't know what to expect.

> **Individualistic example:** Many great leaders were misfits in childhood and even beyond. The same unique qualities that got them in so much trouble in childhood led to contributions to society in adulthood. Think Twain and Edison.

Conservative / Societal
Conservatives like to be with others, and are happier when they are. Their ties to and sense of belonging to organizations and groups is stronger than liberals' as is

their tendency to develop their skills in culturally endorsed ways.

Societal upside: Societies and organizations need a level of citizen conformity and unity for stable growth. If everyone said "I gotta be me" and no one said "you can count on me" there would be no standards to rely on.

Societal downside: Individual strengths can be overlooked when non-conformity is frowned upon. Social norms can erode to the least common denominator without the non-conformist to insist on a higher order.

Societal example: The military is highly dependent on commitment to the social organization. For example, it is apparent from reading *Lone Survivor,* the author Marcus Luttrell's membership as a Navy Seal supersedes his individuality. He repeatedly credits his identity as a Navy Seal for his successes rather than his own efforts.

4. Ambiguity / Certainty

Ambiguity / Liberals
Liberals have a high tolerance for ambiguity and complexity. They can process information for long periods of time without feeling a need to come to conclusions. They are comfortable with nuance and shades of grey.

Ambiguity upside: This tolerance for ambiguity allows for exploration without a need to come to premature, concrete conclusions. It allows the tolerant to wait for things to unfold on their own timetables.

Ambiguity downside: The tolerance for ambiguity can lead to confusion due to lack of clear definition, over-complication due to an unwillingness to simplify, and inaction due to the confusion and over-complication.

Ambiguity example: When voters don't know what a political party or candidate stands for, the party and/or candidate are unlikely to succeed. It also leaves them with the possibility that opponents will fill the vacuum and define them. This was a common complaint about the Kerry campaign.

Certainty / Conservatives

Conservatives like concreteness and certainty. They structure and simplify ideas into their essence.

Certainty upside: Those who prefer certainty can translate abstract ideas into clear, actionable concepts. They are not distracted by erroneous information that can obstruct decisiveness.

Certainty downside: An insistence on certainty can lead to brash actions that ignore subtleties. It can be the bull-in-the-china-cabinet syndrome.

Certainty example: A family member was able to clearly tell me why she supported one political party. She ended her explanation by saying, "I don't really know what the other party stands for." She sided with the side that provided the most certainty.

5. Sensitive / Practical

Sensitive / Liberals
Liberals have active Webby's, emotional brainlets relative to their Izzies, and are sensitive to the impact of decisions on varying groups.

Sensitivity upside: The sensitive can "feel your pain." They empathize and relate to the human suffering of others. They are tuned into the emotional impact of thoughts, words and deeds.
Sensitivity downside: Hyper or unbalanced sensitivity can overwhelm the emotions and lead to avoidance or a lack of objectivity.

Sensitivity example: A friend who appeared on Oprah and many other talk shows to discuss a devastating experience said Oprah was the only one who showed sensitivity to her vulnerability. She refuses to go on other shows anymore, but would appear on Oprah any time. Imbalanced sensitivity can result in poor choices like rescuing an animal that should be put down.

Practical / Conservatives

Conservatives have more active Izzies relative to their Webbys and tend to embrace tough choices unemotionally.

> **Practical upside:** Life involves difficult choices and realistic action. It's important to be able to act without being crippled by emotion.

> **Practical downside:** Unbalanced practicality can result in "objectification," where others are seen as less than human and/or a means to an end.

> **Practical example:** A highly practical person would be more likely than an unpractical one to make difficult choices like sacrificing the lives of a few soldiers for the greater mission. Practicality to an extreme can be cruel.

6. Means / Ends

Liberals / Means

Liberals are process-oriented. They don't just care about where they're going; they also care about how they get there. They relate to the sayings "be the change you want to see" and "life isn't a destination, it's a journey."

> **Means upside:** A means-oriented person enjoys the ride and minimizes the destructiveness of that ride.

> **Means downside:** A means-oriented person can lose a war while arguing over how it is fought.

Means example: Britain was proud of their grace in fighting in the American Revolutionary War, but their elegance made them easy targets.

Conservatives / Ends

Conservatives are results-oriented. They care about getting where they're going, and believe in doing what it takes to get the job done.

Ends upside: This trait can be highly productive. It keeps the eye on the goal and does not allow lesser concerns to derail it.

Ends downside: The "end justifies the means" philosophy can justify means that are worse than failing would be.

Ends example: Destroying a village to save it.

I put these definitions in the book mainly so we can appreciate the qualities of other political leanings. You also can use it to get yourself out of a box someone puts you in. If they have you in a liberal or a conservative box, you can say:

I have the following liberal qualities... and the following conservative qualities... and am always trying to balance them.

Two crooked comparisons

Crooked comparisons contrast groups or individuals in ways that appear to be fair and balanced but are not. When you compare groups and ideas, avoid stacking the deck.

Flexible / rigid

If you're not flexible, does that make you rigid? Maybe —
but it's a crooked comparison — and it's one that
circulated the Internet recently.

A UCLA study examined the brains of liberals and
conservatives and concluded they function differently.
Liberals loved what the study said and made much of it.
Conservatives did not respond well. Why? The study
made crooked comparisons in reporting the results.

Even though most accounts of the study concluded with
the suggestion that liberals and conservatives need each
other, the report was unbalanced in a way that was
objectionable to conservatives and liberals would be less
likely to notice. Here are two imbalances I observed.

> **Unmatched word choice:** The report referred to
> liberals as flexible and conservatives as rigid.
>
> The opposite view would have been referring to
> liberals as "fleeting" and conservatives as
> "steadfast." (I suggest you don't.)
>
> **Uneven extrapolation:** The report extrapolated the
> findings to illustrate the benefits of the liberal
> strength, but did little to illustrate how the
> corresponding conservative trait could have value.
> It said the liberal would adjust more easily if their
> regular route home was closed.
>
> A more even extrapolation would have also pointed
> out how much more likely the conservative would

have been to have established an effective regular route home in the first place. A trait that is adaptive in one set of circumstances could be adaptive in another.

Had the data been reported neutrally, both sides would more likely have embraced the findings. (But of course it wouldn't have been controversial, so perhaps it never would have been reported.)

Brain / heart

Now, I don't believe in false objectivity which suggests that when one side does something, you need to find an example of the other side doing it. In this case, however, there are plenty of examples of compromised comparison on both sides of the discussion. Here's one that created a firestorm.

A few months before retiring from public office in 2002, the House majority leader Dick Armey concluded that "Liberals are, in my estimation, just not bright people. They don't think deeply. They don't comprehend." Armey went on to substantiate his point by talking about how liberals were drawn to "occupations of the heart," while conservatives favored "occupations of the brain," like economics or engineering.

How crooked are those comparisons? Here are a couple of imbalances that I see:

> **Implied assumption:** This comparison equates intellectual function, or analytical ability, with intelligence or smartness. Not everyone agrees.

Assumed values: The remark implies superiority of "brain work" over "heart occupations."

Like the crooked comparisons of the UCLA study, I'm sure assumptions contained in Armey's remarks were inaudible to him — and to many of the people who share his values.

Create your own crooked comparisons. (Really!)
Here's an exercise for you. Create your own crooked comparisons. It will make you aware of your own tendency to create crooked comparisons. You can overcome unwanted behaviors by exaggerating those behaviors. It will help you recognize them when others use them.

Take the trait pairs above that I labored long and hard to align, and create your own in ways that compare the strengths of one group to the weaknesses of the other. For example, instead of adaptable / consistent, you might choose flaky / reliable. Instead of autonomy / authority you might choose critical thinker / gullible.

If you're ready to play with fire, choose pairs like traitor / patriot, or humanitarian / fascist. Hmm — how about bleeding heart / practical? This is just practice, of course — and don't practice on others. The purpose of the exercise is to make you more sensitive to how often discussion magnifies our greatness and their culpability. Be aware – it gets tricky. The sneaky trick is to shade crooked comparisons just enough that they are imperceptibly biased. If you go too far, the alarms go off.

If a manipulator does it just right, the bias slips in undetected.

If someone uses a crooked comparison, you can say:

> *I wouldn't define it as (flexible/rigid.) I'd say it's between being flexible and steady. And yes, I do tend to be steady, sometimes to a fault.*

Two hands for a reason

Okay, did I make it through the comparison chapter relatively unscathed? That wasn't too hard, was it? If you thought your "political opposites" are more useless than poodles (just kidding, poodle-lovers), I hope you've reconsidered.

We have two hands for a reason — to support the progress of the whole. Imagine if your two hands spent the day targeting each other. You'd go hungry! You couldn't afford for that to happen, and we can't afford to be divided as a nation. We need to work together, starting with insisting on honest political dialogue.

Meryl Runion

Chapter 11

*Two sides to every story and
other dualistic deceptions*

Do you ever get tired of duality?

"There are two kinds of people in the world: those who divide the world into two kinds of people, and those who don't." That quote by Robert Benchley says everything you need to know about the limits of dualistic thinking, if you really think about it. But to save you from having to do that, I'll write some more about it.

The liberal / conservative dichotomy is one single dualistic way to define political orientation. I could write a hundred chapters about a hundred other political spectrums we span. You and I could be on opposite ends of some, next door neighbors on others, and within shouting distance on the rest. If we framed our conversation solely in the dualistic definitions of liberal / conservative, we'd miss the rest of the picture. That's the problem with dualistic thinking. Duality means: *being twofold; a classification into two opposed parts or subclasses.* Things that fall outside of the dichotomies don't exist to a dualistic thinker. Once something is classified in one category or another, differentiation is overlooked.

How can any of us have a reasonable political conversation if we're limited to two opposing concepts on any consideration? If an idea is right or wrong? If a party is bad or good? If you're biased or objective?

As for me, I'm biased but work really hard to be objective.

Most importantly, dualistic thinking ignores the big picture. Is the glass half empty or half full? Dualistic thinking picks one. Synergistic thinking says: *yes.* (And of course the engineers point out that the glass is too big.)

At its extreme of political thinking, dualistic categorization concludes: 1) you're either liberal or you're conservative, and 2) one of those categories is good and the other is bad.

After all, we all know there are two sides to every story.

> *"Democracy must be something more than*
> *two wolves and a sheep voting on what*
> *to have for dinner." ~ James Bovard*

Two sides to every story
When two employees don't get along, some managers conclude there are two sides to every story and the truth lies somewhere in between. That's a false objectivity, a logical fallacy called false dichotomy, which they use to dismiss issues as personality conflicts. Sometimes there is equal culpability, but this kind of dualistic thinking prevents the manager from finding out if this is one of those times. This kind of manager might ask a kitten and a wolf in a pen, "Why can't you just get along?" In the manager's mind, he or she is being objective and neutral. Not so.

If you insist that kittens and wolves solve their own problems, you're likely to end up with a lot of wolves and few kittens. Or you'll have wolves and compliant kittens. I've talked with plenty of employees whose coworkers support the "wolf" instead of the "kittens," not out of conviction, but out of fear. It's no way to run an office — or a country.

Dualistic thinking can also show up in the form of assuming one side is all right, and the other is all wrong. A manager might decide that two sides to every story means there's one side worth listening to and one that isn't. They conclude one side is accurate and one is defensive. This is a common way of assessing political issues.

More dualism: the thrill of victory and the agony of defeat Our Izzie attitudes toward winning intensify the dichotomies. We divide the world up into winners and losers. I like winning, don't you? But that doesn't mean I want to live my life like it's a competitive sport where I fight daily to triumph over some hapless loser. It's nice when every conversation doesn't have to be a debate with a victor and vanquished.

Our culture heralds winning. Our culture vilifies losing. If you're not winning, you're "losing," with all the associated mortification that losing implies.

We learn that the world belongs to those who win. Here are some of the "life is a conquest" slogans that many take as a blueprint for living:

- There's a winner and a loser and nothing in between.

- The winner takes all.
- Oh, the thrill of victory and the agony of defeat.
- The majority rules.
- Winning isn't everything, it's the only thing.
- Winning isn't a sometimes thing, it's an all time thing.
- The person who said winning isn't everything never won anything.
- Show me a good loser and I'll show you an idiot.

Do an Amazon.com search on the word *win*, and you'll get 374,378 results. There are books telling you how to win over everything from liberals and conservatives, to diets and fear. There is a strong message that life is a war to be waged and won.

And there's a stronger message that political conversations are wars to be waged and won.

Dualism leads to argument
The win/lose dichotomy keeps us arguing. In her insightful (but rarely inciteful) book *The Argument Culture*, Deborah Tannen explains:

> *The best way to explore an idea is to debate. The best way to cover the news is to find spokespeople who express the most extreme polarized views and present them as both sides. The best way to settle a dispute is litigation that pits one party against the other. The best way to begin an essay is to oppose someone. The best way to show you're thinking is to criticize and attack.*

Ouch. The last two points really hit home for me. They remind me of why I left the academic world after completing college. I sought a new way of thinking and a new way of living. (I found it — you're reading about it here. The new way doesn't negate my old approach, but it certainly augments it.)

Tannen explains that arguing is easier than integrated thinking.

She's right. It is easier. It's a primal trait that doesn't require full brain integration. And because arguing is easier, it's more popular. Because it's more popular, language supports it.

Language favors extremes and argument
Divisive and dualistic slogans, sayings and words outnumber unifying and/or moderate ones. Our language favors extremes and argument.

My marketing consultants suggested ad campaigns for this book with pitches like: "How to talk politics with ANYONE including your enemies," "Insider secrets to have in political conversations with ANYONE," and "the book Washington does not want you to read." Marketers found it harder to come up with unifying slogans.

Think about this: you can look up synonyms and you can look up antonyms, but you can't look up synergyms (words that suggest a balance between two extremes). In fact, I had to invent the word synergym. I look for synergyms constantly in my writing, but there's no official word for it. It's much easier to verbalize one extreme or another of a duality than it is to verbalize the whole or the meeting ground between the extremes.

Unity is the forest. Duality is the trees. If you want to have reasonable political dialogue – in order to be able to ~~incite~~ insight your political other, you need to be able to talk about dividing AND uniting, conquering AND concurring, inciting AND insighting, your opposites AND people who differ somewhat from you.

You need to be able to talk about the whole and the subtleties of the many, many dualities that make up that whole.

Every story is multi-faceted. As long as you pretend there are only two sides to any story, you'll be picking your sides and coming out swinging. And you'll be screaming at each other without accomplishing anything.

Dualistic thinking leads to win / lose dichotomies
The Great Political Divide is really a Great Political Spectrum. So why are most discussions framed as face-offs between the right and the left? Two words: dualistic thinking.

When someone makes a comment that assumes duality, you can say, "Let's not limit ourselves to two options when the world is so much bigger than that."

Chapter 12

*They don't just see things differently,
they see different things*

An entirely different view
One news station covered Katrina by showing extensive footage of stranded citizens on rooftops desperate to be rescued. Another station covered Katrina by showing footage of looting. When their viewers discussed what was happening, they were baffled by the other's responses. They didn't just see things differently, they saw different things.

Forget for a moment what you think of different news sources and just consider how the different exposure provides different foundations for dialogue. If Citizen A assumes Citizen B was as riveted to stranded people on rooftops as she was and didn't see a single looting clip, Citizen' B's words would be baffling.

I was in Australia when the Iraq war began. I watched the news on CNN International, which covered the war differently from CNN US. I watched the same war as my friends and family back home, but saw an entirely different view. I still augment my news consumption with international news sources, and I still remind myself that most people I talk to do not access those sources, and are not interested in starting.

Why would a reasonable person act this way? One of my favorite communication books (beside my own) is Crucial

Conversations. The authors recommend that during conflict, you should ask yourself the following question:

> *Why would a reasonable, rational and decent person act this way?*

For political conversations, you can ask:

- *Why would a reasonable, rational and decent person think this way or say what they're saying?*
- *What information or influences are they exposed to that I am not?*

This question makes an assumption that we rarely make in political dialogue. It assumes the person who disagrees politically is a reasonable, rational and decent person. They might not be, but it's useful to start with the idea that they could be.

You can never accurately infer intent from action. (It's called the fundamental attribution error.) Too often we attribute ill-will. It can help immensely to instead assume good will and proceed with curiosity from there.

Curiosity, not condemnation
Curiosity suspends judgment, and that makes it a powerful tool in political communication.

I confess; there are people I respect who have expressed political opinions that strike me as uninformed, dangerous and inconsistent. These are intelligent people and it baffles me that they hold the opinions they do. Surprise! They think the same about me! That's the way it usually works.

Start the curiosity process by putting on your magic eyes in an effort to see what the persona who differs from you politically sees, and how differently they see it. Remember, this is information gathering. Ask questions inspired by your curiosity. You're wondering:

- *Why would a reasonable, rational and decent person think this way?*
- *Do they see things differently or do they see different things?*
- *What can I learn about them from looking at what they see?*
- *Can we explore each other's sources from the same side of the Political Divide?*

Here are some things you can ask:

- *I see it differently. What do you base your opinion on?*
- *Where do you get your information about that?*
- *What do you like about that source?*
- *How reliable has that source been for you overall?*
- *Have you ever found that your source misrepresented facts?*
- *Do you believe everything your source says?*
- *Your source and mine differ in how they tell that story. Why do you suppose that is?*
- *Do you think your source presents a balance of perspectives?*
- *Your source criticizes (people of my political leaning.) Does knowing me make what he says seem more or less accurate?*

- *Do you think your source's descriptions of (other groups) are more accurate than the way these groups represent themselves?*
- *I agree with your source about...*
- *I feel uncomfortable that you get your information exclusively from (source) because I don't agree with the way s/he characterizes my position. Does that make sense?*
- *I'd like for you and I to keep each other posted on what our sources are saying. Are you open to that?*
- *What else do you think?*
- *What other perspective do you think people have about this?*

I know, you've probably already discredited their sources. You've probably already tracked down 30 of the most outrageous things they've said and found them to be fictitious or fallacious. That will make it harder to stay open to seeing what they see. But if you want to ~~incite~~ insight your political converse, it helps to see what they see. In the negotiation chapter of my book *PowerPhrases!,* I show how when you can describe someone's position better than they can, you gain credibility and therefore influence. You get respect when you give it; respect breeds respect.

Giving first is a great way to get
It's amazing how often people want others to understand their perspectives, but they are unwilling to reciprocate. It's a universal principle; you get what you give. Sure, you can ask for someone to see what you see, but if you haven't led the way by stepping into their reality you're unlikely to inspire them to want to step inside yours.

Chapter 13

Houston, we have a systems problem

A set-up of a different kind

Pigs are set up these days. They're getting a bad rap. Yes, I'm talking about the pink oinkers that most of us only encounter as ham.

You see, pigs are very sweet-natured animals. At least they're sweet in their natural environment. But the way they're raised these days doesn't draw out their sweetness. I once knew a man who spent his days on a pig farm factory cutting off pig tails. That was his job, because the pigs were in such close quarters that if he didn't cut the tails off, the pigs would bite them off. You probably didn't want to know that, but I had to tell you to make my point.

Tail biting is not normal pig behavior — or shall I say that's not normal pig behavior in normal pig environments. Most pig farms are anything but normal piggy environments.

I facilitate difficult conversations, so if I could get the pigs talking, here's how some of it might sound. Porky would say:

> *Hey, Babe, I'm sorry I bit your tail off. It's really not you. I got so frustrated from how cramped it is around here I took it out on you.*

Babe would share his experience and let Porky know he wished he had better impulse control so he (Babe) would still have his tail. He then would shift his focus to how he would prefer to be treated in the future.

By the end of our facilitated discussion, Babe and Porky would have stopped blaming each other, realizing both are reacting to their close quarters, not to each other. They would establish coping behaviors to deal with their mutual system-imposed predicament.

That wouldn't solve the problem, but it would help them deal with it. Babe and Porky still wouldn't have control over the environment that stressed them, but at least they wouldn't be blaming it on each other.

Systems problems are a set-up for people problems

Babe and Porky have what Management Guru W. Edwards Deming called a *systems problem*. They are in a situation that sets them up for conflict. They take their frustration out on each other, when the issue is with the dysfunctional system.

Deming suggested that 85% of the issues groups face are due to the system, not the individuals. I suggest that's a conservative estimate.

As a trainer, I often am called in to address issues that turn out to be caused by a systems problem. For example:

- When managers are supposed to be working cooperatively but are evaluated competitively, they have a systems problem.

- When one overworked administrator supports twelve managers, each of whom thinks their work is most important, they have a systems problem.
- When honest vendors can't close a deal because other vendors cheat, they have a systems problem.
- When clean athletes can't compete because the competition uses steroids, they have a systems problem.
- And when our airwaves are filled with people screaming at each other but not saying anything, when some are claiming to do no wrong and others to do no right, and when we find ourselves screaming at our families, friends and neighbors the same way, we have a systems problem.

The echo chamber

You hear talking points every morning. Pundits and politicians repeat them throughout the day. By evening your neighbor parrots the attacks verbatim as if he or she has always used words like "out of the mainstream" or "rampant obstructionism." (It's odd when you hear the language of the day from individuals first, and later discover it was the verbal flavor of the day for their party.)

I don't know about you, but I think that's a problem.

It's a systems problem. Sure, you can blame the ditto-er for his or her distinct lack of critical thinking, just like you can blame Porky for biting Babe's tail off. I suggest you cut them some slack and work on coping skills. Most importantly, don't bite their tails off in revenge. Learn how to respond instead of react. The trickle down needs to stop somewhere, so let it stop with you.

The serenity affirmation

I recently conducted training in an organization that turned out to have some serious systems problems. After a period of complaining, I redirected the conversation to a discussion of what I think is the most powerful wisdom on earth. You'll find it in the Serenity Prayer. Since this was a government organization, I secularized it and turned it into a serenity affirmation. You can use it either way.

The Serenity Prayer says: *God, grant me the serenity to accept the things I cannot change, the courage to change the things I can, and the wisdom to know the difference.*

The Serenity Affirmation says: *I have the serenity to accept the things I cannot change, the courage to change the things I can and the wisdom to know the difference.*

We have a systems problem regarding our political communication. We are unlikely to change that.

But we can change how we respond. And perhaps if enough people do, the system will eventually change.

Stop your whining

I've heard people incite people politically by telling them to stop their whining. Often the "whiner" is voicing a legitimate complaint and the critic characterizes the complaint as whining to undermine the complainer and avoid addressing the message. However, even the most unfair accusation usually contains a hint of good advice.

When you complain, know what you hope to accomplish by it. If you are just whining, move toward action. Don't waste your time and energy in "ain't it awfulling." Stop complaining about things you can't change and go about taking action regarding the things you can.

I often tell my seminar attendees to stop their whining, but I say it in a much nicer way. I redirect their attention to potential action, and once that's exhausted, we focus on coping skills.

Kind of like Porky and Babe.

Washington, we have a political communication systems problem. If that leaves you feeling powerless, stop your whining. No, not because there's no reason to whine. Do it because that will free your time and emotional energy for where it can do some good. Whining only indulges in what you cannot change.

Be an agent of unity and resolution, not divisiveness and despair.

Systems problems don't excuse bad behavior

Please don't get me wrong, as many people do when I say complaining wastes precious energy. I am not telling you to shut up about injustices, abuses and genuine issues. I'm not saying people who lie, cheat and game the system are innocent victims, either. I'm telling you to invest your words wisely, stop doing what doesn't work, and start doing what does work. If that means taking productive action to change a dysfunctional or corrupt system, I applaud you. Make your decisions with your eyes wide open and decide what battles you will take on.

When you feel bogged down in whines and complaints, you can say:

> *I agree it's a mess. One thing I do to contribute to upgrading the level of our political communication is... How about you?*

In the next chapter I describe your options and ways to take the serenity prayer / affirmation to the next level and know what your true alternatives are.

**Pick battles big enough to matter,
small enough to win. ~ Jonathan Kozol**

Chapter 14

Say what you mean, and mean what you say,
without being mean when you say it

Democracy depends on dialogue

Do you censor yourself because you're afraid you'll be attacked or ridiculed if you speak? Do you shut people down who disagree with you? Do you say what is expected or what others want to hear rather than what is on your mind and truly important? Are you unaccustomed to speaking truth to power? Are you afraid to rock the boat?

Are the political waters so muddied that you want to disown all things political?

If only we could make our problems go away by ignoring them. If only I could have made my late husband's cancer go away by ignoring it.

But it doesn't work that way. Sometimes you need to move through the mud to get out of it…alive.

When people don't know what to say, they usually say nothing

There are eight reasons that people use to justify not speaking up when something needs to be said. The reasons can be valid; however they are often just "Lame Excuses" that perpetuate secrecy and dishonesty.

The reasons are:
1. Misplaced respect for authority.
2. Fear of negative consequences.
3. Not wanting to offend.
4. Avoidance.
5. Habit.
6. No one else is saying anything.
7. Self doubt.
8. Don't know how.

The ultimate communication formula

If you can't remember hundreds of phrases, communication tips, techniques and communication formulas, just remember to: *Say what you mean, and mean what you say, without being mean when you say it.*

That's been my ultimate communication formula for years. Hardly a week goes by without someone telling me that this simple phrase has made an enormous difference for them.

It's simple elegance is what makes it so powerful — for personal and political conversations.

The formula speaks for itself, but I'll go into more detail anyway.

Say what you mean
Say what you mean. Isn't that obvious?

Well, no. In fact, many people don't even think of saying what they mean. It's more than that. Most people are so conflicted and confused they don't know what they mean.

Rather than think deeply, some wait for the next sound bite to form their opinion for them. Some are so busy looking for a winning argument that it never occurs to them to look for words in their own meaning.

So, what do you think, what do you feel, and what do you want? Figure it out and talk about it.

Truth is far more compelling than hollow talking points.

For example, I saw a man on a shuttle reading a book that had a title that was inflammatory toward the political group I identify with most. We struck up a conversation, and he tried to sell me on the author.
- I thought: why would I want to read an author who demonizes my ideas?
- I felt: antagonized.
- I wanted: to explore alternate views without having mine attacked.

When my friend was irate over the wording of a political ad:
- I thought: she was right to object, but was losing sight of the bigger picture.
- I felt: polarized by the intensity of her condemnation.
- I wanted: to defend the advertisers, but more than that, I wanted a more balanced discussion of the bigger picture behind the ad.

When another friend went on a political rant about something that happened 30 years ago while thousands of US citizens were standing on New Orleans roof-tops begging to be rescued from floods:

- I thought: his focus was misplaced.
- I felt: aghast.
- I wanted: him to care.

When a newsletter reader caught a minor error in a post I made on my blog and used it to discredit my entire point:
- I thought: he's playing gotcha.
- I felt: minimized.
- I wanted: him to play fair.

That's what I thought, that's what I felt, that's what I wanted, and that's what I said. For example, I told my shuttle buddy: I don't understand why you would think I would want to read a book that basically calls me stupid in the title. I find the author antagonistic, and would like to be able to explore alternative views without being personally attacked.

It was refreshing and effective.

Mean what you say
Mean what you say means speak with conviction. Conviction comes from clarity and leads to courage.

Conviction
The most compelling speakers are those who speak with conviction. They know what they mean and mean what they say. The second you parrot someone else, you've lost your authenticity. If you use talking points or language that isn't your own, you'll come across as false. It's okay to quote people who say what you want to say and say it well, but don't let their words come out of your mouth

pretending they're yours. Put your own thoughts into your words.

Use "The Five C's of Responsible Leadership

CLARITY results in conviction: a clear commitment to your beliefs.

CONVICTION inspires courage: The "courage of conviction."

COURAGEOUS leaders are willing to use candor in their communication.

CANDOR lends itself to creative expression.

CREATIVE expression adds clarity to your position. *(Source: www.SpeakStrong.com)*

Take the time to clarify your own thinking to enhance your conviction. Any "fuzzy thinking" and "fuzzy feeling" will weaken your conviction and thus your clout. Get as certain as you can be so you can mean what you say.

Weak speak
Next, eliminate weak speak that suggests you don't mean what you say. Some very passionate people speak in ways that suggest they aren't. Here are some kinds of weak language you need to watch out for:

1. Eliminate filler words (um, uh, etc.) one by one.

2. Don't choose to excuse your words. Stop apologizing for having an opinion.

3. Interrupt your interrupters. It's not rude to interrupt those who interrupt you. Let people know you want to finish what you have to say and once you have, you'll listen to them.

4. Replace passive voice with active voice.

Don't: talk like the subject is the object, unless the subject really is on the receiving end. Structure your sentences as subject / verb / object — or someone does something to someone.

5. Avoid words like "kinda" and "sorta" and "a little," and "I was thinking maybe," and "I just have one little point" that signal you don't mean what you say. Words like "I know you're not going to believe me" discredit your words before you speak them.

6. Address dismissive attitudes. Mention it if they seem closed to what you're saying.

Back words up with action

Mean what you say decrees that you back your words up with action. You walk your talk. You put your words into motion. You do what you say you will. You protect the power of your words by matching your walk to your talk.

It's obvious what this means for elected officials — it means they honor their campaign promises. But what does it mean for you?

It means if you set communication agreements with someone, you follow them. It means if you set communication agreements with someone and they don't follow them, you say something. It means if you say you will not use or tolerate a certain kind of language, you don't.

Don't be mean when you say it
Many people say they like my Ultimate Communication Formula until I get to this part. This part of the formula balances out the first two parts of the ultimate communication formula.

Because we often think and communicate in opposites, many people think if they're not passive, they're aggressive. They think if they're not aggressive they're passive. The word "assertive" is often confused with aggression.

"Don't be mean when you say it" doesn't mean you make nice, avoid unpleasant truths or back off at the first sign of resistance. It means you use diplomacy and lose the barb. It means you respect the person you're talking to.

Here are some things for you to avoid:
1. Sarcasm
2. Labeling
3. Blame
4. Emotional manipulation
5. Threats
6. Yelling
7. Sideswipes, pot shots, sniping
8. Personal attacks
9. Passive-aggression

10. Playing "gotcha"

It means you embrace:
1. Accuracy
2. Honesty
3. Solutions
4. Points of agreement
5. Listening and discernment
6. Substantive information
7. Accountability
8. Courtesy
9. Respect
10. Objectivity

How to "insight," not incite others

It's pretty simple really. If you want to talk to all three brainlets, which is what you would do in a reasonable discussion, address the foundation of all three brainlets.

Address what they and eventually what you:
- Think (The Prof)
- Feel, (Webby)
- Want. (Izzie)

Express:
- Reason (The Prof)
- Emotion, (Webby)
- Action (Izzie)

Talk in terms of:
- It, (The Prof)

- We, (Webby)
- Me (Izzie. Their "me," or them.")

Don't just talk to one of their brainlets. Talk to all three.

Political think / feel / and want

Here's your challenge. The next time someone offers a political comment that triggers you, no matter how inflammatory it is, listen and reflect until it is clear to both of you that you fully understand what they think, feel and want.

Then, and only then, tell them about what you think, feel and want.

That's how you upshift a conversation so you can navigate the great political divide in a way that insights, not incites.

The technique works with gender divides, it works with generational divides, it works with style divides and with patience and time it works with political divides.

Stay tuned. There's more.

Chapter 15

Bust the bully…and stop playing the victim

"Trust and verify." ~ Ronald Reagan

Losing control

Have you gotten over your control fantasies?

- Do you enjoy dominating, victimizing, being perpetually right, controlling, intimidating, disparaging or provoking reactions in others?

- Do you manipulate to get what you want and overpower people who say things you don't want to hear?

- Do you catch yourself thinking, acting and talking like an oppressor, dominator and vanquisher?

How about the victim side of control?

- Do you ever get a peculiar pleasure out of being subtly or overtly dominated? Does self-pity and playing the "innocent victim" ever melt your butter? Do you insist on fighting losing battles and relish blaming others for your choices?

- Do you let people manipulate you, silence you and provoke reactions in you that leave you "beside yourself"?

- Do you catch yourself thinking, acting and talking like you're oppressed, dominated and victimized?

How about when the topic gets political?

When it comes to politics, all bets are off. When the topic gets political, Izzie emerges. Even the wisest among us succumb.

Like a psychologist whose work I studied while researching for this chapter. I'll call her Dr. Ellie. I spent several hours on her extensive and beautiful website about victim-abuser behavior. I found Dr. Ellie's articles to be insightful and her comments to her readers to be wonderfully supportive. This, I thought, is an objective woman who understands balanced, assertive communication.

Then, I found an article in which Dr. Ellie compared the moral character of two politicians. Now, all bets were off.

Dr. Ellie's post crookedly compared the dignified goodness of one politician to the abusive badness of the other. She did not just label behavior, she labeled the men. She characterized one as *The Buddha* and the other as *The Abuser*.

Dr. Ellie supported her character claims on discredited allegations. The charges were proven false more than five years ago. She wouldn't have had to look very far to check her facts and discover her error. Two commenters told her exactly where to go for clarification. She never acknowledged that in her attempts to bully her detractors into silence. She dished it out and couldn't take it.

It gets worse.

When many of Dr. Ellie's readers took issue with her comparison, Dr. Ellie stopped communicating and started arguing.

She psychoanalyzed the emotional state of some of the commenters. She made remarks like: "Another angry person." "I wonder what you're really angry at." The "angry" posts sounded reasoned to me, but even had they not been, I would have preferred a response based on the merits of their arguments instead of the delivery.

She turned tables using straw men counter-attacks. When a commenter listed some unprincipled things *The Buddha* did, Dr. Ellie did not address the issues raised, but instead countered with a list of unprincipled things *The Abuser* did. Her response a) did not address whether the list undermined her *Buddha* characterization, and b) argued as if the poster wrote to defend *The Abuser's* behavior, which he did not.

She abandoned the rules of discussion. Dr. Ellie complained about the political nature of the responses she received, insisting that her post was "an editorial and not political." Yet she made her own political commentary throughout the comment section when it served her arguments.

She was entrenched. There was no appearance that she had considered, listened or explored any of their points and there was no evidence she questioned whether there could have been a flaw in her post or responses to commenters. Even factual evidence was dismissed without consideration.

Dr. Ellie sidetracked. She changed the subject from content to delivery even when the delivery was beyond reproach. For example, she told one commenter: "I respect your opinions and thank you for writing. Why? You come from a place of reason and modulated emotion. You have not made the too common mistake of allowing yourself to be ruled by impulse and emotion. Here's a lesson gang: whether or not she was inflamed at reading my editorial, she 'sat on it' long enough to express her disagreement well." Yet Dr. Ellie's response ignored the content of the post.

Dr. Ellie's approach was not only unreasonable, it was ineffective. The more she argued, the less she convinced. What happened to this infinitely wise woman whom I had spent hours admiring?

The answer is: the topic turned political.

Subtle domination

Dr. Ellie's responses contained subtle domination. To put this in perspective, I'll tell you that we all subtly dominate at times. And we all play victims at times too. Although I detail the domination tactics Dr. Ellie used in her responses, I don't consider Dr. Ellie to be a dominator in general. I surmise that the topic of politics activated a defensive and aggressive response in a woman who is generally reasonable. Political dialogue can bring out the very worst in the very best of us.

A few names of domination games:

1. Absolutes
Absolute language is dominating language. Absolute talkers define issues in black and white terms and do not acknowledge the existence of gray. People who think and talk in absolutes control by presenting a false-dichotomy which distracts the listener from considering options. It limits the debate to alternatives suggested by the absolute thinker. If someone asks me if I prefer Coke or Pepsi, I may not consider the options of water or carrot juice.

A few commenters on Dr. Ellie's editorial objected to the "blanket generalizations"... as did I.

It is hard to differ with an absolute thinker / talker because:
> 1) They consider one argument is right and the other is *wrong*. Being wrong is too painful to consider, so the *right* response is defended beyond reason.
> 2) They don't recognize nuanced arguments. Arguments are for or against a monolithic position.
> 3) They don't recognize conditional arguments. You're with them or against them.
> Some absolute, domination words to monitor are: always, never, every, worthless, useless, biased and

any. Look for words that imply that incidents are all pervasive and permanent.

Respond to absolute language by mirroring back the absolute nature of their comments. For example, say:

- *Are you suggesting there are only two options here?*
- *Am I correct in hearing that because I question the latest reports on X, that you regard me as biased, and therefore you dismiss anything else I say?*
- *Do you consider those isolated behaviors to define their overall character?*

Talk about the use of absolute language itself. Say:

- *That's a false dichotomy. Let's explore the full range of choices.*
- *You're painting with a broad brush. Do you see the situation as cut and dried as your words imply?*
- *You use the word always (etc.) Do you mean that literally?*
- *Worthless is a strong and absolute word. Are you claiming that there has been no value at all in this program?*
- *I get the impression that you're upset because I don't agree with everything you say. Am I right?*

True dominators / absolute thinkers are unlikely to respond to any kind of rigorous thinking, but those who have been polarized by the absolute nature of the national dialogue might.

2. Personalization

Another way to dominate is to personalize conversations. The victim personalizer treats challenges to ideas as personal attacks. The bully personalizer attacks the character or qualifications of the commenter rather than address points on their own merit.

Dr. Ellie leveled several personal comments instead of addressing their objections on a factual, logical or substantive basis.

Respond to victim personalization by addressing the dynamic and/or the impersonal nature of your comments. Say:

- *I'm not questioning you; I'm questioning the point.*
- *I'd like to argue with you, not against you.*

Respond to attacking personalization by refocusing the conversation to the issues at hand. For example, say:

- *I suppose I am frustrated, because I see the situation as urgent. However I'd like to focus on the facts rather than on my state of mind.*
- *If I come across as angry to you, we can talk about how I might word my concerns differently. However, for now, I'd like to hear your responses to the substantive points of the discussion.*
- *I don't think it's appropriate to change the subject from the issue to my state of mind. Let's not get personal here.*

People with victim tendencies often are silenced by personalization either to avoid offending someone who personalizes their opinions, or because they feel discredited by attacks. Address the dynamic by saying:

> - *Do my challenges to your position on this seem personal to you? I don't intend them to be, so if there's anything I do that makes this personal, please let me know. Otherwise, let's stay on topic.*

3. Yeah, but you (they)

Turning the tables is an effective way to dominate. For example, if a husband complains about his wife spending too much money on Christmas, she might "yeah-but-you" him by talking about his car. The car may be a legitimate issue in another context, but not when she uses it to take the heat off herself about her own spending. While table-turning occasionally has a legitimate function of identifying a double standard, more commonly it is an avoidance tactic that blocks dialogue.

When a scandal breaks out in one political party, party leaders drag out scandals from the other party that sometimes date back as far as forty years and beyond. What's sad is, predictably, your neighbor will echo these distractions.

When you're "yeah-but-you'd," say:

> - *That may be, and if you want to discuss that later we can bring it up then. Now, I'd like to discuss the point I raised.*

- *I'm not suggesting perfection on either side. Right now, I'm exploring the appropriateness of this situation.*

4. I write the rules
Have you ever played a game with someone who wanted to rewrite the rules as they went?

If you control the rules of a conversation, you can dominate it. Simply accuse others of breaking your communication rules instead of addressing the issues. Since you're in charge of the rules, you can break and change them whenever it serves your purposes.
Address this by saying,

- I don't remember agreeing to those rules. I'm happy to negotiate communication agreements with you that we both can follow.

I detail setting agreements in Chapter 21.

5. Labeling and name-calling
Oh, do I dislike being labeled, and I do have to watch my own communication to avoid doing it myself.

One of my most memorable experiences with labeling was a business partner who labeled me "selfish" when I didn't do what he wanted. It seemed the reverse of reality, but it did get me doing a song and dance for a while to prove his label wrong. (Now I think I should have embraced the label. I could have used some more selfishness.)

I was stunned the first time someone labeled me as belonging to a specific political group. I felt summarized, condensed and dismissed. It was as if everything I had said became secondary to the prejudged label. I also felt misunderstood, because I didn't think I belonged in the box they put me in. It told me they hadn't been listening to what I said.

From "wacko" to "pinhead" to "idiot," labeling is rampant in the world of political dialogue. Yes, Dr. Ellie did this one too, when she called the politician she didn't like an "Abuser." Whether he earned the label or not, the use of the label reduced this man to one negative quality. Labeling specific behavior can have its place. Labeling an entire person, argument or point of view is reductive and destructive.

When you are labeled in a political conversation, if the shoe fits, wear it proudly. You can clarify, expand on or redefine the label. Say:

- *What do you mean by (label?)*
- *If by (label) you mean (your definition) I accept it.*

If you don't like a label, say so. Say:

- *I disagree with your characterization of me. It makes me think you're dismissing me.*
- *If you consider me a (label) either I'm not clear, you're not listening or both.*

If a label is truly offensive, say:

- *I will speak to you with respect and I expect you to do the same for me. That label does not show me the respect I deserve.*

6. Dominator infallibility
Some people are addicted to "being right." If there's a problem, it's the other person's fault. If someone disagrees, the other person is wrong.

In the meantime, everyone else gets to be wrong.

Suspending judgment and balancing advocacy with inquiry opens dialogue. However, if you or the person you're speaking with prefers to dominate and prevent dialogue, you can do that by acting infallible and ignoring any merit in opposing arguments.

Address dominator infallibility by asking:
- *Are you open to the possibility that we could learn from each other?*
- *Are you open to the possibility that I might have something to offer this dialogue?*
- *I don't think the policies or candidates are perfect, and I don't think the ones I don't support are without any merit or positive qualities. Do you think your polices and candidates are perfect?*

Infallibility disempowers the fallible. Someone who habitually responds to input by proving themselves right and others wrong leaves others feeling weakened (or angry.) If you suspect you are dealing with dominating tactics, take your clues by noticing whether you feel like a peer or subordinate.

I recently spent a day with a minor celebrity whom I respect and admire. I was surprised by how disempowered the day left me feeling. While on the surface, he was supportive and generous, I ended the day feeling ineffective. When I reviewed the day, I caught scores of subtle domination cues. The ultimate test of how balanced relationships and interactions is: *how safe and empowered do you feel?*

I asked myself how empowered I felt when I considered the idea of addressing my concerns to Dr. Ellie. I wanted to recommend her site to my readers but was hesitant to do that since her post seemed (mildly) abusive.

> **"He who establishes his argument by**
> **noise and command shows that his**
> **reason is weak." ~ Michel de Montaigne**

I realized I was hesitant to email her because she had been so dismissive and hostile with others. I did not see any evidence to suggest she would be open to my input.

I emailed her anyway, and have not received a response.

Healthy, reasoned political dialogue leaves all parties feeling empowered.

A note to passives — don't be a victim or a volunteer:
As a recovering victim, I used to blame the dominant people in my life for overpowering me. That got me nowhere…besides widowed.

It took me a while to recognize the ways I allowed myself to be silenced, dominated, oppressed, etc. It took me a while to recognize how freely I took my responsibility for my own life and handed it right over to other people, as if to say, "here, you deal with it. I don't want the responsibility." That way, I got to blame someone else when it didn't work out.

I'm over that now. Are you?

The dominant voices in our political dialogue aren't necessarily the wisest ones. Blaming them will get you as far as blaming my late husband got me.

This is your life, and you are responsible for it.

This is our country and we are responsible for it.

Anyone who stays silent and gives dominators free rein shares responsibility for the outcome.

A note to aggressives:
Don't be a victim of your own aggression. If you think aggression works for you, I'll say this:

> *Sure, you can get the more timid among you to cower to your bully pulpit. You can get the gentler souls to back down. You can win short-term goals.*

> *You can silence people, just like my late husband silenced me when I was concerned about his health.*

You can win...and lose everything in the process — just like he did.

Don't be a victim of your own aggression. Let other voices be heard. This is *how to restore sanity to our political conversations.*

A note to passives and aggressives:
Lose the language of: the oppressor and oppressed, dominator and dominated, vanquisher and victim. Give up the games and have genuine conversations. Stop arguing and start communicating. Move from debate to dialogue.

Reasonable dialogue uses language that is based on a symmetry and balance. Those qualities provide you with more power than dominance ever would.

Chapter 16

Twelve tips to untangle twisted logic

Spin doesn't just trickle down

They call it political "spin" for a reason; it twists facts and confuses issues in order to unfairly influence opinions, beliefs, and decisions. Washington pundits and politicians have mastered the art of spin, and while I won't take a stand on the trickle-down theory of wealth, I will definitely take one on my trickle-down theory of spin. Spin doesn't just trickle down to personal conversations, it flows there. Before the debate is over, our family, friends and neighbors consciously and unconsciously parrot the party lines of their party of choice.

How NOT to respond

When something strikes you as propaganda, here's how you don't respond.

My friend Sandra is dating a career military man named Brent. Brent sent Sandra a sentimental You Tube video clip about remembering our servicemen.

Sandra was so turned off by the piece; she told Brent that she "couldn't listen to the whole thing." She dismissed it as pure propaganda and told her beloved to: "Give me a break."

I'd call that a blanket dismissal, wouldn't you?

Her complete rejection polarized the conversation. It sent Brent to the other side of the fence and the finger-pointing fest continued for a few days.

Perhaps the video exposed essential differences in core values they each hold. Their debate never became a dialogue that allowed them to discover what they were really arguing about.

However, it was less intense than some of the polarizing comments on the YouTube page, where condemnations escalated to death wishes.

Sandra's Izzie was activated and she was unable to stay open enough to acknowledge any value in something Brent had found so meaningful. If she had, chances are Brent could have stayed open to what Sandra found problematic. Instead, he accused her of being cold.

A kinder, gentler approach is a more effective one.

Here are some tools for your twisted logic untwisting toolbox.

1. Stay calm
I read a sign on an elevator about what to do in case of an emergency. I was surprised by how it began. It started:

Step One: Stay Calm

I thought, "that's a step?"
Well, actually, yeah, it is.

And it's your first step to untwist twisted logic.

By staying calm, you tame Izzie long enough for the Webby and The Prof to kick in. If you don't stay calm, you are likely to speak in a way that is satisfying in the moment, but doesn't get results. If something someone says makes you so angry you can't let them finish their sentence, they're not the only ones lacking in reason. You are too.

The classic warrior strategy treatise *The Art of War* contends that whoever is not calm has already lost the challenge. If no one is calm, your conversation is doomed.

Sandra let her Izzie agitate her into communicating in a way that alienated the man she loved. That might not be why he left her, but it probably contributed.

She could have said something like:

> *I'm reacting to it and want to wait until I've had time to respond instead to comment.*

"Nothing gives one person so much advantage over another as to remain always cool and unruffled under all circumstances." ~ Thomas Jefferson

2. Get over "gotcha"

Okay, one more attitude consideration before I get more specific. Get over playing "gotcha." Give up playing a game of finding mistakes and rubbing the other person's nose in it. Sure, you see the gotcha game all over the news.

Feigned outrage fills the airwaves over gaffes – perceived or otherwise. But your goal here is reason and understanding, not scoring points. We're changing the game, remember? Get over "gotcha." Even people who are careful with facts make factual errors. If you pounce on one like a toddler on an Easter egg, they'll become defensive.

To build trust and openness, overlook minor factual errors that don't change the conclusions anyway, and challenge the significant ones in ways that allow them to save face. Sandra cold have said something like:

> *This is the kind of thing I usually don't care for because I feel manipulated. But since I love and respect you, I'm open to the idea that I'm missing something.*

3. Respond in your own language, not theirs

I recently saw a news clip of a young Pakistani protesting to protect "certain unalienable rights." Clearly she was passionate about her protest, but her word choice made her seem like she was mimicking rather than communicating. She came across as adorable, but as a protester that's probably not the effect she was going for. Her own words would have served her better.

So pick your own words, and pick them with care.

For example, let's consider the YouTube video that Sandy said she couldn't finish because it's *pure propaganda.*

Propaganda is Sandy's word. If Brent uses Sandy's characterization and argues it is not propaganda, he will be in a defensive win-lose dichotomous argument. Instead, he should use his own language in his response.

For example, he might refer to the video as a soldier's advocacy piece, or a tribute to service personnel.

He can reference the "tribute" without highlighting the word change, or he can say:

Instead of propaganda, I think of it as a tribute.

Whenever anyone trivializes your perspective, find your own words to best express your view. Political parties name bills, issues and agendas, but only you can find the language that represents the way you think about something. The more original and authentic your wording, the more powerful your communication will be – so don't talk about certain unalienable rights unless that's really how you think and talk.

4. Address hidden agendas
Here's a new word definition for you. "Foreploy: Any misrepresentation about yourself for the purpose of getting laid." (This comes from a Mensa Invitational which asked readers to change one letter in a word and create a new definition. Their words, not mine).

"Misrepresentation about yourself for the purpose of getting laid" is a hidden agenda. So is misrepresentation about the issues for the purpose of winning a political argument.

133

If the words and stated intent don't match up, address it. You can never Restore Sanity through counterfeit communication.

The main hidden agenda you are likely to encounter is a desire to win disguised as an invitation to reasonable dialogue. If, after you present a heartfelt explanation of something that matters very much to you, you discover that the person who presented as interested was actually only looking for ammunition to undermine you, say so. You can say:

> *I shared sincerely and as factually as I know how in the spirit of collaborative dialogue. Your response leads me to believe that you're more interested in winning an argument than exploring and looking for truth. Can you understand why I might think that?*

5. Expand false dichotomies

Do you like dogs or cats? Are you an inside person or an outside person? Do you play it safe or take risks?

Were those questions valid or bogus?

I presented options as if they were mutually exclusive. I gave you false choices. People do it continually.

I mentioned the false dichotomy that *Crossfire* hosts Carlson and Begala struggled with when Jon Stewart implored them to engage in civilized dialogue. They kept asking if they should be harder or softer on their guest, and didn't consider alternatives.

A man I met on a shuttle gave me false choices that were more like no choices. He said, "You don't like Hillary, do you?" Not only did his question limit my options to liking Hillary or not liking her, the way he asked the question made it clear he disapproved of anyone who liked Hillary.
If someone asks if you believe in free speech or censorship, or if a YouTube video is propaganda or a moving tribute, you can answer:

> *Yes!*

Or you can expand the false choices into real ones, as I did with the man on the shuttle. I said:

> *My response is more complex than that, and I'd delighted to explore it with you if you have the time.*

We arrived at the terminal, and he changed the subject.

"Dichotomy begins with a certainty that eventually leads to enduring doubts while dialogue begins with doubts that eventually lead to enduring certainty."
~ Leland R. Beaumont

6. Clarify abstractions

Do you support the troops? Do you love America? Is freedom important to you? Security? Values? Fairness? Integrity? Motherhood?

Hey, sign me up for all of the above!

Are you against corruption, injustice, abuse, evil, enemies, free rides, traitors, waste and hypocrisy?

Well, yeah, I want on that list too.

But just what do these abstractions mean?
Remember the email Brent sent Sandra with the link to the soldier video? The email was sent to a list with the words: "If you don't support the troops, delete my email from your contacts list."

I've spent hundreds of hours conducting training on military bases, and they keep asking me back, so apparently I support the troops enough for them. But I'm not sure if I support them in a way that qualifies me for Brent's contact list.

When someone raises abstractions, ask for specifics. Debate specifics, not definitions. Ask:
- *What does (abstraction) mean?*
- *Can you give me examples?*
- *Please be more specific.*

- *That's an abstract concept that can mean very different things to you than it does to me. What does it look like specifically?*

That will add substance to your conversation.

7. Consider systems

Someone initiated a conversation about the Abu Ghraib scandal during training I conducted on a military base. Clearly, not a single person in the room believed the abuses were caused by a few bad apples. They saw the situation as a system that endorsed the behavior and scapegoated those who implemented orders.

Many issues are caused by bad systems. I read a satire about a "delusional" presidential candidate who actually believed telling the truth would get him elected president. Pretty crazy, huh! Heaven help us if someone that nutty was elected! Yes, politicians are responsible for their own distortions. Considering systems is not the same as giving people a pass. It means looking at situations realistically.

Speaking of systems, think about the steroid abuse issue. Sure, players who use them are culpable, but in an environment where everyone or almost everyone uses them, players who don't use them are at a serious disadvantage. So why does the recent report focus exclusively on players and overlook the owners who had to know?

It's a systems problem. The people who like the system the way it is have more power to influence investigations and reporting.

We live and work within a variety of systems. The family, the marriage, the democracy, capitalism, the transportation system, the political system, the media systems, the education system, the health care system, the tax system, the legal system, the government agencies. Often your conflicts are the result of a poorly designed or implemented system.

When you and someone else seem to be on the opposite sides of the political fence, consider what system you are both in and how the system rather than the people in it are contributing to the conflict. You could be like Porky and Babe in Chapter 13, fighting each other because the system sets you up for conflict.

You may not be able to change the system. But, ignoring a system and focusing solely on those who work within it is a certain way to perpetuate the system. Say:

> *I'd like to talk about the system that drives this behavior.*

At the very least, you will accurately consider your genuine options instead of blaming individuals who are caught in a dysfunctional system.

8. Check the facts

Everyone knows that if you flush a toilet in the southern hemisphere, it will spiral in a different direction than if you flush it in the northern hemisphere.

Everyone knows that the Great Wall of China is the only man-made object visible from the moon.

Everyone knows that men think about sex every seven seconds.

Everyone knows those things, and everyone is wrong."

Politics are rife with false "truths" that everyone knows. After all, the guilty don't need to prove their innocence; they just need to create doubt about their guilt. The unscrupulous don't need to prove false charges against their political adversaries. They only need to create questions in the electorate's minds. Whisper campaigns do that insidiously and effectively.

So check the facts. Do you know that one of the cable news stations won a lawsuit on the basis that there is no rule or law against distorting or falsifying the news in the United States? No kidding!

So before you accept a claim that "everyone knows" is true, go to the source, read the transcripts, examine the bills, watch the videos and research on snopes.com and factcheck.org. Question the track record of your favored sources to see how their information has withstood the test of time (or not) and even research claims by sources that you find generally reliable.

Don't be an agent of misinformation or disinformation. When you are faced with existing misinformation, correct it calmly, kindly and factually. Say:

> *I'd like to pool our knowledge on this topic because we have access to different information. I've researched this topic and some of your information is flawed. Here are the facts I've uncovered.*

Act as a firewall by refusing to let rumors propagate through you. It can open a great dialogue or end a bad one quickly.

> *You're entitled to your own opinions, but you're not entitled to your own facts."*
> *~ Senator Daniel Patrick Moynahan*

9. Reflect defective thinking

A few years back, Ms. Teen South Carolina gave an unintelligible response to a question about why the Americans can't find the US on a world map. While I can't guarantee I'd shine under her circumstances and I take no joy in the avalanche of ridicule she endured, I will say I'm relieved that no one pretended her rambling gibberish was logical. In contrast, some "fedspeak," fuzzwords, gobbledygook and political spin that defies logic is treated as if it made sense.

The next time someone says something spurious that masquerades as logic, don't pretend it makes sense, but also don't attack like many did after Ms. Teen South Carolina's gaffe.

Mirror what they say back to them so a) their own words hang their argument, b) you can clarify whether they really mean what their words imply and c) if you don't have a clue what they're trying to say, you can find out instead of guessing. Say:

- *Are you suggesting that...?*
- *Am I hearing you right that...?*
- *Is your point that...?*
- *Let me make sure my understanding is clear. Are you saying that because of... (blank) will happen?*

Then take it to its logical implications:

- *If that's true, wouldn't it mean that...?*
- *Are you saying that those of us who think X are mistaken?*
- *Do you think my skepticism is baseless?*
- *Are you suggesting that I don't know what I'm talking about here?*

Hey, you might as well get it out on the table!

Work to identify the premise and the conclusion and the logic that connects them, if any. Examine the evidence presented to support each premise. Explore the things that genuinely confuse you. Remember, your purpose is not to expose them as an idiot, but to try to answer the question, "why would a reasonable person think what they do?"

10. Highlight the agreement first, disagreement second
I knew I was listening to political radio but I wasn't sure what kind. The host introduced the hourly news report by

saying, "I'll be back after you've listened to the lies on the news." A network news report followed.

Even polar opposites agree on some things. Both sides of the political divide think the media is dysfunctional. They just happen to think the other side controls the message at their side's expense.

Here's a real surprise: There are more people who believe the sun revolves around the earth than trust big business. Distrust of big business often crosses party lines.

Find where you agree before you launch into where you differ. I like asking:

Where do you think we agree about this?

It gets us considering similarities and collaboration.

Then you can move into areas of disagreement. Begin with specifics.

- *I don't entirely disagree. Here's the argument than counters your argument. I'd like your impressions of it.*
- *At some levels you and I agree. I have respect for your position. Let me explain what seems like a bigger issue for me.*
- *We agree in many areas. There's one area where I find myself yelling at the TV – I'd like to get it on the table and move on past it.*

11. Augment, don't argue

When someone tells you you're wrong, what's your reflexive response?

Yeah, me too. I like being right. I particularly like it when I actually AM right, but I like being right even when I'm wrong, too. We all do.

That's why you are usually better off augmenting, not arguing with differing political opinions.

Okay, there are times when you need to tell someone they're way wrong, but usually they'll hear you better if you say "yes and" instead of "yes but."

But wait. Am I telling you to tell someone they're right when they're not?

Nope. It's different than that. It's a fine art called "acknowledge without agreeing." I use it in every seminar I teach. I provide a boatload of phrases to use when you do it in my book *PowerPhrases!*

"There is something valid in every position."
~ Johan Galtung

Here are a few *Power Phrases* for you:
- *I hadn't considered that.*
- *The point you make about ___ hits home.*
- *That's an interesting perspective.*

- *I didn't realize people were looking at it that way.*
- *I think about it differently.*

Then, instead of refuting, say:

- *Have you considered...?*
- *Are you aware that...?*
- *Here's another angle...*
- *Yes, and...*

Ask for some kind of confirmation for what you've said. Don't ask for agreement unless you think you're likely to get it. Seek simple acknowledgement. For example:

- *Can you see how I could see it this way?*
- *Does that make sense?*
- *Have I explained it clearly?*
- *Is there anything I just said that you relate to?*

Remember, you're not going for a victory here. You're going for seeds of understanding. Celebrate any progress you make in that direction.

12. Be as strong as you need to be (and no stronger)
While I always recommend starting gently, there are some bullies in the world that only respond to sharp rebukes. Sharpness can create resistance, and unless you must make your point immediately and are certain the other person regards gentleness as weakness, your best approach is to be as strong as you need to be and no stronger.

Bluntness may be effective when a more considered approach fails. If a considered approach does not succeed, add some sharpness and see if it earns the respect of someone who had interpreted your cooperative and collaborative approach as weakness. Let them see your resolve and unwillingness to accept nonsense or be intimidated. Escalate gradually as seems needed.

Unlike Stewart, I wouldn't call Tucker Carlson or anyone a "dick." But Stewart probably had a better sense of how big a wakeup call his audience needed.

13. Consider the walk-away option
Steven Covey is famous for describing *7 Habits of Highly Effective People*. His forth chapter is: *Think Win/Win*. That principle asserts: If we can't find a solution that would benefit both parties, we agree to disagree.

Negotiator Roger Fisher and William Ury take it one more step. They say, *Very often if a win-win cannot be achieved, going for a no deal could be the best answer.*

It's what you call walk-away power. You don't have to engage in an abusive dialogue. If your political-other seems determined to conquer, simply say:

- *This isn't working. Let's not do this. I'd rather just discuss the weather with you. Perhaps we can revisit this later and see if we can be more open to each other then.*

It may not be ideal, but it's honest. And it will save you from a lot of bruises. Sometimes all people need to change from adversarial combative diatribe to civil, cooperative dialogue is to know that you have the strength and willingness to set and enforce a boundary by disengaging. You always have the power to walk away and decide to readdress it another day.

You have the power — but not the kind you think. When the logic twists and turns, give up the hardball tactics that invite attack. Also, give up softball tactics that invite abuse. Be pleasantly persistent, annoyingly reasonable and clearly willing to enforce the boundaries of reasonable dialogue.

You have the power and it's a kind of power worth having.

Chapter 17

Don't get fooled again – logical fallacies

Aggression's Law

When I was a teenager, I used all kinds of strange logic to justify my bad behavior. My dad was/is a logician, but sometimes he capitulated to excuses from me that didn't pass the smell test. I don't think I fooled him. I think I wore him down.

Kind of like how much of our political dialogue works.

Was logic on my dad's side? Sure, but so what? I won the battles I was determined to win. Persistence trumped logic. It often would have been better if it hadn't.

Aggression is like that. Aggressions' Law says that erroneous arguments drown out accurate ones. Unprincipled diatribe drives out reason. She who is most ruthlessly committed wins. (It's really Gresham's Law, but since "Aggressions' Law" is sexier, I'm using it.) I learned as a teen that manipulation, pressure and nagging worked! I learned as an adult that I had to find another way. We all do.

Even smart people are fooled and or beaten down by logical fallacies, especially when Aggressions' Law triumphs over reason in the public domain. If we continually hear logical fallacies treated as if they add up, who can blame us for losing our discretion? If the media adds 2 and 2 and gets 5, who can be expected to remember what it once equaled?

I detail ten of the hundreds of logical fallacies here. No, I'm not describing them so you can use them to win arguments and alienate people. You probably already use them to do that. (And you probably don't know you do it because we tend to believe our own press.)

I detail them so you can avoid using them yourself and you can spot them rather than be blindsided when they come at you. I detail them so you can get people to discuss politics fairly rather than falsely. And if understanding logical fallacies helps you to have a reasonable dialogue with your teenager, (no, I'm not dreaming) I won't complain.

Common fallacies and fallacy-busting phrases

Trust me on this…there are far more logical fallacies than you want me to detail here. But this list will give you a great beginning. It's a bit like riding a bike. Once you get the gist of it, it gets easier.

Here's a tip. Whenever possible without sounding too weird, call a fallacy by name, especially the ones with Latin names. It sounds official, and eventually others will learn what the fallacies are. With any luck, they'll stop using them.

If you can't get "argumentum ad superstitionem" to roll off your tongue as if you say it every day, just refer to their claim as a "logical fallacy."

1. Slippery slope
(runaway train, overall generalization)

If dad sets a curfew time, his teen accuses him of moving toward not letting her go out at all.

Slippery slope arguments suggest that a small step in any direction will lead to planetary destruction and/or global depravity.

- *If we lower the drinking age by two years, we'll soon be lowering it by ten.*
- *If I help my husband with his chores one time, they'll all become my job. If I eat one potato chip, I'll eat the whole bag. (Yes, occasionally there is some validity to the slippery slope argument.)*
- *A small modification to a bill is the first step toward demolishing it. So watch out, because you know political action is like eating potato chips.*

Respond to slippery slope arguments by saying/asking:

- *That's a slippery slope argument. It's a fallacy. I could just as well suggest if you have a glass of wine at a party, you'll end up a homeless drunk. I credit you with more discretion than that. (Don't use this analogy with someone in AA.)*
- *Are you actually suggesting that any move toward (A) will inevitably lead to (Z)?*
- *Are you really afraid that (A) will lead to (Z), or are you suggesting that because you don't want (A)? (If they seem actually like they are...)*
- *FYI, I don't know anyone advocating (Z), or even (MNLO or P.) This really is only about (A).*

- *What evidence do you have that supports the suggestion that if we implement (A), (Z) is inevitable? I'm not advocating Z, I'm only suggesting A.*

Of course a journey of a thousand miles begins with a single step, but that doesn't mean that anyone who takes a single step is likely to travel a thousand miles. Oh, that could be a phrase for you too!

2. Straw man argument

If mom wants her son to study more, he accuses her of sabotaging his social life and wanting to control him.

Straw man arguments misrepresent the other's position in ways that are easy to dispute, and then argue against a claim or request that no one actually makes.

- *If you suggest someone made inappropriate comments, they argue against random censorship.*
- *If you support, say, relaxing prison sentences on certain offences, they argue against emptying the prisons.*
- *Politicians and pundits are quick to let people know what "the other side really wants." It's usually news to liberals to hear that they "want failure in Afghanistan" and news to conservatives to hear they "want a conservative presidential dictator."*

The arguments are distractions from real issues.
Respond by saying:

- *That's a straw man argument that misrepresents (the conservative) (the liberal) (my) position. Please take the time to understand what I'm suggesting before you explain why I'm wrong.*

- *You're not going to succeed in convincing me by attacking an argument I haven't made. Let's talk about what I'm actually saying.*
- *That would be a reasonable objection if I was arguing X, Y and Z. I'm not Here's my actual point.*

3. Argumentum ad hominen (attack the messenger)

The parent is fifty four which is over the hill. No matter how relevant his or her comment is, it will be discredited by discrediting the parent.

- *If you can't attack the argument, attack the arguer.*
- *If your spouse suggests an investment is unwise, tell him/her they don't know enough to assess it. That way you don't have to explain why it is a prudent investment.*
- *If you offer a suggestion in a meeting, they explain you haven't been there long enough to know how things work. They never do explain why the idea won't work.*

Republicans and Democrats consistently dismiss each other's points on the basis that the other is inherently "biased" rather than on the merits. A satire once suggested that Hillary Clinton argued that Obama wasn't qualified to be president because he wet the bed as a toddler. That is a satirical version of a common fallacy.

The attacks both distract from and undermine the valid arguments. Respond by saying:

- *Please address the idea rather than my (or my candidate's) qualifications to make it. Even idiots make good arguments sometimes, so I'd like to know what you think of the idea, not of me (the candidate).*
- *You're right. I don't know what it's like (to be 18 these days.) But that doesn't make my concerns wrong. Please tell me why it's okay for you to (questioned behavior), not why I'm not qualified to object.*
- *Are you attacking me because you don't have a good response to my point?*

If you want to sound erudite, say:

- *That's an ad hominen fallacy. It attacks me and does not address the argument. It is unacceptable. Please withdraw your personal attack on me and address the substance of my argument.*

If you use the word "ad hominen" in a general setting with people who are not familiar with the word, do it playfully.

4. Argumentum ad populum
(everyone agrees, bandwagon, tyranny of the majority)

Marcie and Barbara's parents are letting them go to the concert.

Who wants to be left out? Millions, thousands or even just hundreds of people couldn't be wrong, could they? Uh, yeah, but don't expect that to stop anyone from claiming they can't.

- *Everyone stays out into the wee hours of the morning so it must be okay.*

- *More people have PCs than Macs, so PCs must be better.*
- *There was a rush to buy a stock called Enron, so it must have been a great buy.*
- *Most people drink Coke or Pepsi, so they must be okay.*
- *No one else is alarmed by the recent legislation, so it must be benign.*
- *Candidate A is "out of the mainstream" so everything Candidate A says is flawed.*

Just because "everyone" agrees doesn't mean it's right. In the popular game show "Who Wants to be a Millionaire," contestants can ask the audience for their opinion. Sometimes the audience gets it wrong.

If popular opinion determined reality, the earth was flat during the Middle Ages, but now it's round. (Sounds like a very unsettling transition.)

Respond by saying / asking:
- *Are you suggesting that the popularity of your idea affirms its correctness?*
- *I like to make my own decision based on examining the merits of a position, not on who else does or doesn't support it.*
- *You're using the logical fallacy of argumentum ad populum, or the bandwagon argument. Let's talk about the actual idea instead of how popular it is.*

Of course, parents often counter "proof by popular opinion" by saying, "If everyone jumped off a bridge, would you?" This rhetorical question sounds condescending and is flawed because the chances that everyone will decide to jump off a bridge are slim. But it does make the point that we need to decide for ourselves.

5. Argumentum Ad Misericordiam
(Argument from pity, appeal to emotion)
You should be able to afford a private school for me, because I hate the school I'm in.

Oh – those heartstrings! They can lead you to some very illogical choices! Webby is a good contributor to any conversation, but her input needs to be balanced with genuine logic.

- *You need to acquit Joan for the crime because if you convict her, her children will grow up without their mother. (Wait, her being a mom proves she's not guilty?)*
- *Bill deserves a raise because he has three kids in school. (Uh, um, how do Bill's kids determine the market value of his work contribution?)*
- *The situation is unacceptable. We cannot tolerate the problem. We must continue our efforts no matter how costly because people are suffering. (So we should keep a policy that isn't solving the problem going because if we don't, the problem won't get solved? How about some evidence that the efforts are actually working to solve the problem?)*

Respond by saying / asking:

- *I care about (X, Y and Z), but the fact that the situation is tragic doesn't prove (their point.)*

- *Insanity is doing the same thing and expecting a different result. If we really care about (pick your problem) I suggest we talk about something that hasn't already proven itself ineffective.*
- *You're using the logical fallacy of Argumentum Ad Misericordiam, or appeal to pity. I do care about the situation, but my empathy doesn't blind me to the fact that there are some flaws in your claim that we need to address.*

Pity is only one of many emotional appeals. Other emotional appeals are to: fear, flattery, ridicule, guilt, hatred, fear of humiliation and spite. They all use emotion in lieu of reasoned arguments, and even suggest emotion is a better guide than reason. I'm a big fan of paying attention to emotion, but to support reason, not override it. Emotional appeals are manipulative fallacies.

6. Petitio principii (Begging the question)
Kids should get their licenses when they turn sixteen. I turn sixteen next week so I should get my license next week.

Begging the question is an argument that assumes a premise that is based on the conclusion.

- *Lying is wrong because we ought to tell the truth.*
- *We should intervene, because that's the right thing to do.*
- *Only civilized nations can be allowed to have nuclear capacities. The civilized nations are the ones to decide which nations are civilized.*

Respond by saying,

- *I'm a big fan of truth-telling, but this is not an honest argument for it. Let's look at some of the advantages and disadvantages of lying and come up the real reasons to be truthful.*
- *It sounds like you're saying we should intervene because we should intervene. I'd like evidence. Let's examine the pros and cons of intervention.*

7. Unwarranted assumptions

Unwarranted assumptions are sometimes confused with begging the question. Someone presents an assumption as fact (for example, assuming a "B" is a good grade) without evidence supporting it and draws a conclusion based on the assumption. Here are some examples:

- *We know the policy worked because even the (liberal) (conservative) media reported that it did.*
- *Since it is (isn't) our responsibility to spread democracy around the world, we should (shouldn't) overthrow the dictatorship in (country.)*

Respond by identifying the assumption and examining its validity.

- *I don't agree with your assumptions that the media is (liberal) (conservative) so your argument doesn't convince me the policy worked. Please give me more concrete evidence of its effectiveness.*
- *I don't accept the premise that it's our role to police the world. That's not an argument that will convince me to approve the overthrow of foreign governments.*

8. One-sided assessment (Cherry-picking facts)

One-sided assessment emphasizes the pros of the ideas it favors and the cons of the ideas it does not.

- *If you get me a car, you won't have to drive me around all the time.*
- *We should pass this bill immediately for the following thirty reasons.*
- *If we enforce this law, the following bad things will happen.*

One-sided assessment is common in public discourse and is the basis of our legal system. One-sided assessment is not a fallacy when there is an opportunity for the opposing views to be equally represented. Our legal system is based on one-sided argument with the premise that both sides will be argued effectively and truth will out. Of course, if a well-staffed team of shrewd attorneys handle the defense and an overworked public attorney handles the prosecution, chances are one side will get a far better representation and logic will not prevail.

One-sided arguments assume equal competence and representation in the arguing of both (all?) sides of an issue. That assumption is rarely borne out.

One-sided arguments often favor short term gains that go uncontested because there is no one from future generations to argue their interests.

During Mick and Cindi's divorce, Mick made one-sided arguments about what was fair distribution, and Cindi tried to reason both sides. Guess who got the better deal!

If someone you have a reasonable amount of trust with uses one-sided assessment, try to bring them around to honest dialogue by saying:

- *Yes, (I wouldn't have to drive you around.) Let's put that on the pro list in our considerations. Then we can look at the cons.*
- *Now that we've looked at the upside of this bill, what limitations to you see?*
- *What are the negative consequences of not enforcing this law?*
- *Even though you argue your case very well, I'm actually more skeptical than I was before. Your arguments seem one-sided, which diminishes my trust. There must be some downside to this proposal.*

Call for balanced arguments before calling for a decision.

9. Shifting the burden of proof
Prove me wrong
This fallacy makes an assertion without proof, and puts the onus of disproving it on the other person. That allows for bogus claims without supporting evidence. Rules of logic put the burden of proof on the person making a new claim rather than the one who questions the new claim.

The space shuttle Challenger is said to have blown up because a manager insisted, "You can't prove it will fail, so we should go ahead with the launch."

Here are some examples:
- *I think you're hiding money from me. Prove that you're not.*

- *They intend to harm us. It's up to them to prove that they aren't.*
- *My opponent did not serve honorably. I challenge him to prove me wrong.*

Respond by saying:
- *What do you base your claim / accusations on? It's unreasonable for you to make a claim without evidence and ask me to prove you wrong. Let me know what you base your claim on and we can examine that.*
- *Extraordinary claims require extraordinary proof.*
- *You're asking me to prove a negative, and that's not my responsibility. I invite you to provide positive evidence of your claim.*

10. Wishful / magical thinking
It must be true because I want it to be.
This fallacy assumes a happy ending and goodness because we want it to be. It considers hope to be a strategy. For example:

- *I don't believe Joe did that because I don't want to think someone in my family would behave that way.*
- *Don't worry, it will all work out. It has to.*
- *We'll be able to turn the economy around because if we don't, it will be a disaster.*

A clever response that you may not want to use but to keep in mind is:

If wishes were horses, beggars would ride.

Some others are:

- *Wishing doesn't make it so. What is the evidence?*
- *I'd like some concrete indicators that this will turn around, not the fact that we want it to.*

In general, ask for specific evidence and a specific plan.

There's more where that came from. There are hundreds of logical fallacies. I'll stop at ten. Pay attention to the arguments people use with you, and see if any of them fit the definitions of the fallacies listed here. If they don't, continue your research.

The simplest approach to fallacies is to ask yourself: does that argument make sense? When an argument seems disingenuous, twisted, rigged, oversimplified, or in some other way false, step back and ask yourself – what doesn't add up? Is the evidence irrelevant or unrepresentative to the conclusion? Does the argument ask you to accept an assumption that is not self-evident to you? Have you gone from a collaborative inquiry to an adversarial one?

Don't let Aggression's Law spoil your logic
When you are faced with a logical fallacy, if you're not sure how to respond, remember your ultimate communication formula: say what you mean and mean what you say, and don't be mean when you say it.

What do you think? What do you feel? What do you want?

You can always say:

> *I don't follow your logic. Let's go through it in more detail.*

Elaborate with:

What is your conclusion, what are the premises you base that on, and what is the evidence supporting those premises?

Although there are an unlimited number of ways to argue incorrectly, there are only a few ways to construct a valid argument. Insist on using valid forms.

If the people you speak with are willing to work with you, set some communication ground rules to guide your dialogue.

Chapter 18

Negotiate ground rules for your political conversations

Rules set you free

Most counselors, mediators and coaches provide "fighting rules" for their clients. It's kind of *like Robert's Rules of Order* or parliamentary procedure for interpersonal conversations. It keeps discussions productive, minimizes hostility and makes it safe to talk.

That's the theory anyway. You might watch the Senate operate and wonder how effective the procedures are, but on the other hand, at least they don't break out into fist-fights like parliaments in some countries.

Procedures can be manipulated – and will be if those who enter into them do so without sincere intent. Ground rules work best if you've both had it with quarreling and are genuinely interested in resolution, not domination and capitulation. You know – if you actually want to relate instead of debate.

Here's an example of what guidelines do. If I know my husband isn't going to ridicule me for my opinion, I feel much safer voicing it. If he knows I'm not going to play gotcha with him by rubbing his nose in an innocent error, he feels safe speaking without planning every word to make sure he doesn't give me ammunition. But mainly, if we both know we're in it together, on the same team, working together, we both feel safe and free to explore.

And that's the seeming paradox. Rules will set you free. So call a cease-fire and come up with agreements that will get you and your people with opposing views dialoguing like cohorts. Effective rules and guidelines create openings for reasonable dialogue.

Rules on the fly
If you can't stand back and set up a series of agreements, it doesn't mean you're back to the old games. It just means that you'll have to be more skilled from your own side. I heard a radio host named Richard establish rules of dialogue during a few minute call.

I'll call the station "Star Radio" to keep my communication point clear. "Herb," a supporter of the "Stripes" party called in, and began by saying, "I hope you'll have the decency to let me talk, unlike other Star Radio hosts who hang up on me and don't let me have a chance to talk."

Richard agreed to let Herb speak. I suspected the other hosts had hung up on him for good reason and Richard was living dangerously by promising to let him have his say. I listened with interest.

Herb launched into a rant that started with, "You Stars are idiots if you believe a fraction of what you're saying." He continued with name-calling, insults and unsubstantiated personal attacks. There was no substance in his comments.

Richard handled the call with restraint and diplomacy. For example, he told Herb:

I'd like for you to call in every day, but in order for that to happen, I need you to let me respond to your comments. Can you agree to that?

Herb did agree. He did interrupt Richard later in the conversation at which point Richard reminded him of his agreement.

I wondered, *Does Herb really think he should be able to dominate, be provocative, make personal attacks and the host should just sit there and take it?*

Apparently he did, but Richard managed to get him to agree to a few interaction rules as the conversation progressed. Richard got the caller to agree to symmetry in their conversations. I was impressed.

So take some pointers from Richard. If it's not the kind of situation where you can collaborate on a whole set of agreements, propose a few as you go.

Customization
Richard's guidelines evolved from the needs of the conversation. Your best conversational guidelines will be customized based on your own dynamics.
My logical husband and I have customized guidelines for our conversations. For example, I've learned to warn him when I go off on a tangent so he doesn't even try to connect it to what I said before.

When you set your rules, consider the ways your conversations are derailed and what guidelines can keep you connecting.

Intent

Examine your intent. Do you really want to stop arguing and start communicating? Or are you attached to winning? Can you give up the idea of being right and them being wrong? Are you committed enough to, say, help them make their point, rather than exploit their inability to verbalize it?

In my flash movie *A World of Truth*, I ask viewers to imagine a world where "as a child you could talk about anything, grown-ups took time to listen to you, and when you were upset with someone, they helped you to find the words to talk about it." That's the kind of interaction I'm talking about here. Yeah, it includes helping them successfully tell you they think you're doing wrong.

What have you got to lose?

After all, the real commitment isn't just to them – it's to the truth and constructive dialogue.

If they are ill-informed and delusional, we'll never convince them of their folly by dismissing them.
If they have one side of a multi-sided story, we can learn a few things and so can they.

The only thing we have to lose is ignorance. Oh, yes, and pride, ego and your own delusions. We're better off without them.

Set the intent by saying (and meaning):

- *I'd like for us to stop arguing and start communicating about politics. I'd like to work like a team and look at politics from the same side of the fence. I'd like to hear what you have to say and for you to hear what I have to say. Are you open to that?*

- *Let's establish communication guidelines to do that.*

We're on our way!

Recommended statements of intent:
Here are some guidelines you can start with and adapt to your own needs:

1. We agree to work together to exchange ideas and learn from each other.
2. We wish to honestly influence the other and are willing to be influenced by one another
3. Everything we say will support our intent to *Restore Sanity to Our Political Conversations.*
4. We will assert our own positions on the merits of valid arguments.

RECOMMENDED GUIDELINES:
Define the issue in shared problem terms.
Good phrase:

> *We will address our communication challenges as our problem discussing politics with each other rather than*

assuming the other is the source of the problems.

Pick battles.

Avoid arguing for the sake of arguing. Address questions that move you toward the core of the issues. Leave the candidate haircut conversations for your discussions with people you agree with.

Good phrase:

> *We will avoid tangential issues that distract from important issues and encourage the other to do the same.*

Invite openness.

Good phrase:

> *We will invite each other to speak openly and authentically and show respect and interest when they do.*

Speak respectfully.

Good phrase:

> *We will speak with respect, and make every attempt to understand. We will assume good will until evidence suggests otherwise. If one of us feels disrespected, we will respectfully address that.*

Avoid loaded language.

"Wing nut" and "fascist" are out.

Good phrase:

> *We will avoid and adapt emotionally charged language. If one of us is offended by a term, we will use that to explore the wound behind the term.*

Break when the intensity becomes uncomfortable.

Like when we start to see horns growing out of each other's heads.

Good phrase:

When things get heated and we find ourselves reacting instead of responding, we will break.

Acknowledge when the other person convinces us of anything.

Good phrase:

When one of us is influenced by something the other says, we will acknowledge it with phrases like, "I hadn't considered that, "you make an excellent point," and, "I said I'd allow myself to be influenced by you, and you just changed my thinking a bit."

Be gracious when the other person acknowledges our points. Avoid saying: *Hooray! You finally see how superior I am.*

Good phrase:

When the other acknowledges a point we make, we will be gracious and sensitive about the need for face-saving.

Provide evidence for assertions when asked.

Good phrase:

When one of us asks the other for reasons for our conclusions, we will honor the request and explain why we reached the conclusions we did.

Discuss one subject at a time.

Good phrase:

If a discussion of one topic raises tangential topics, we'll part the new topic until we both feel satisfied with the result.

All conversation is conducted as between equals.
Good phrase:

> *We share our expertise without pulling rank. We will use our expertise to clarify the issue, not disqualify the other to offer input.*

Have a conversation about conversations if the dialogue turns to debate.
Good phrase:

> *When it feels like we're speaking at cross purposes we'll shift the focus to how we are dialoguing and get back to constructive conversation.*

Acknowledge if one of us slips into trying to win through aggression or manipulation.
Good phrase:

> *If one of us catches themselves slipping into aggression or manipulation, we will admit it.*

Apologize, excuse and move on when one or both breaks the agreed guidelines.
Good phrase:

> *When one or both of us speak in ways that violate the agreement, we will admit it and move on.*

Listen without countering.
Interrupt only when needed to clarify what the speaker is saying or when one dominates the conversation.
Good phrase:

> *We will allow each other to complete our thoughts, letting the other know if their point is too long or complicated to be digested as offered.*

Give your listener time to respond.

Good phrase:

> *We allow each other to respond. If one party seems excessively long-winded, we will set time limits.*

Affirm areas of agreement throughout the discussion.

Good phrase:

> *We will keep note areas of agreement and emphasize them as useful.*

Seek to agree, but be willing to agree to disagree.

Good phrase:

> *When we reach an impasse, we will agree to disagree and move to other topics.*

Thank each other for information.

Good phrase:

> *We will acknowledge the gift that the other gives us by sharing their thoughts and ideas.*

Play with it.

Play with your guidelines, but take them very seriously. You and your political other just might find out you have more in common and in complement than you knew – if you can only listen to each other long enough to do that.

Chapter 19

Switzerland, Snopes, Neutrality and You

How do they do it? Switzerland managed to maintain neutrality through every single war in the 20th and the 21st century.

If you think complete neutrality isn't possible, you're right. Humans by nature have a point of view. So when I talk about neutrality, I'm not talking about absolute neutrality. I'm talking about doing our best to suspend our judgment and walk in the other person's shoes, and regard the information in front of us without judgment.

People act like *any* kind of neutrality is impossible in politics. Sure, it's difficult, just like it's difficult to listen to someone complain about your behavior with the same neutrality that you listen to them complain about a stranger's behavior. That doesn't make it impossible.

The Swiss haven't maintained their neutrality by accident. Their constitution declares *preservation of Switzerland's independence and welfare as the supreme objective of Swiss foreign policy.* Switzerland isn't randomly neutral – it's deliberately and fiercely neutral. As a result, Switzerland hosts a plethora of international organizations and has maintained bilateral associations with many conflicting factions.

I'm not suggesting that Swiss-style neutrality should be your goal. I am saying that you need to know what your supreme objectives are, and deliberately and fiercely commit to them. And if I've done my job so far, your supreme objective in dialogue is to stop arguing and start communicating.

So think Switzerland. And be you.

Then there's Snopes

Snopes.com has its own brand of neutrality. Snopes.com has become the gold standard for verifying or debunking urban legend and common fallacies – including political legends and fallacies.

Unlike Swiss-style neutrality that does not take a position, Snopes-style neutrality takes very clear stands, according to criteria it evenly applies. It classifies information as true, false, disputed, mixed, or things that could have happened but are unverifiable.

Swiss-style neutrality says, *it's all the same to me.* Snopes-style neutrality says, *I differentiate according to standards that I apply uniformly to everyone.*

The ACLU (American Civil Liberties Union) has a Snopes-style neutrality. It defines itself in terms of its commitment to first amendment rights, equal protection, due process, the right to privacy and extending rights to traditionally disenfranchised segments of society. While their foundational principles generally align them with the political left more than the political right, they have also defended the civil rights of conservatives Sean Hannity, Rush Limbaugh and Senator Larry Craig and sponsored suits to protect the civil rights of the KKK.

The NRA (National Rifle Association) knows what it stands for too. It will protect gun owner's rights whether the owner leans left or right.

Think Snopes. And be you.

And then there's you
Switzerland, Snopes.com, the ACLU and the NRA have clearly defined who they are and what they stand for in clear and understandable terms. Have you? Or do you call yourself a liberal or a conservative and leave it for the rest of us to decide what that means?

The words "liberal" and "conservative" have become so vague that we all have our own definitions. If you tell me you're one or the other, I might think I know what you mean, and I might be completely wrong. In fact, we could label ourselves as "political opposites," only to discover that we're actually pretty closely aligned.

If the political landscape wasn't (in)conveniently divided into left and right – if there were no established political categories, how would you define yourself politically?

Once you know what you stand for, you'll stop fighting anyone else's wars – and protect and promote what you really believe deserves your protection and promotion.

And then there's me
Here's my commitment: I believe free, open and honest political dialogue deserves protection and promotion. I want a world of political truth where we choose between substantive options, not irrelevant packaging. I want bills

in the legislature to have titles that reflect what they actually do. I want accountability of those with political power to be the norm, not the exception. I want government that responds to all the people, not the loudest few.

I want to be able to talk to my neighbors about political issues without us looking at each other like we have horns on our heads. I want to read political articles, blog posts and comments, and to learn something without having to sift through diatribe.

While I have opinions about Iraq, Iran, Israel, Katrina, immigration, tax code, media consolidation, lobbyists, corporate regulation and oversight, my defining political issue is the need for constructive, authentic communication. I honestly believe that if we can clean up our conversations, we will be able to make the kind of informed political decisions our democracy requires.

Communication is the supreme objective of my political endeavors. Even if I like a policy, I don't support anyone lying to promote it, and I will let them know.

And back to you
Take the time to define yourself. Know what matters most to you. Know what you would put in your own World of Truth video. Determine the ways your perspective is unique to you and the ways it is similar to others. Create a 60 second response to the question: "Which way do you lean politically?" And take the time to learn how to talk about it in a way that will interest more than alienate people when you share your political perspectives.

Think of it as a political first date. Smart daters don't lie, but they also don't open by confessing the most controversial aspects of their histories. They get to know each other before they share their deeper secrets. They learn each other's language and values so they can speak in ways that the other is more likely to understand.

You probably don't start your first dates by listing the things you don't like about the opposite sex; you don't make your case by starting your political dialogue by complaining about groups the other persona might identify with.

Just like a savvy woman wouldn't suggest her new companion read *Men Who Hate Women and the Women Who Love Them* or *No More Mr. Nice Guy,* you probably shouldn't start your conversation with your new liberal friends by suggesting they read *If Democrats Had Any Brains They'd be Republicans* nor should you suggest your new conservative friend read *The Conservatives Have No Clothes.* Those are things you work into as you develop trust — although I suggest you never work into anything more inflammatory than informative.

Neutrality is not false objectivity
In my management seminars, attendees are often relieved to hear that they don't have to treat all their employees the same to be fair — they just have to apply the criteria and standards the same. People actually write that down as if it's a revelation. If they reward one employee for a great job, they don't have to reward lesser performing employees. To think that you do is false objectivity of

177

balance. If the standard for rewards is performance, true objectivity evaluates the performance irrespective of who the performer is.

In a precious paragraph before last I listed a title targeting Democrats and a title targeting Conservatives. I didn't have to do that to be balanced. In fact, doing that was a bit unbalanced. It took me a few seconds to find titles that implied Democrats are idiots, evil and corrupt. It took me much longer to find an "appropriate" inflammatory title targeting Republicans. There just aren't as many.

Don't get me wrong. There are plenty of inflammatory titles that slam Bush, the Republican Party and Republican spokespersons such as Ann Coulter. But I had a difficult time finding titles that attack the conservative you're likely to have a conversation with. Book titles lead me to believe the right is more willing to attack the liberal *base* than the left is of the conservative *base*.

Does that claim make me unbalanced? Not at all. It's a reasonable conclusion based on evidence. If you present me with valid contradictory evidence and I ignore it, then you can call me unbalanced.

Neutrality doesn't mean that you equally endorse or condemn everyone. It means you apply reason and standards the same way across party and ideological lines. Neutrality means you suspend your point of view long enough to consider, listen, understand and explore alternatives, assert your point of view, and revise your perspectives according to reason.

Chapter 20

Common political conversation infractions

All bets are back on

Remember what I told you earlier about how when it comes to political conversations, all bets about reasonable dialogue are off? Well, they're back on – with new skills and rules. Just because our national political dialogue is insane doesn't mean yours has to be.

My readers have submitted six kinds of political communication dilemmas. This chapter suggests responses to each.

1. Assumed agreement

Meryl,

I belong to a group in which most of the members are on one side of the political fence, and I'm often on the other. These are people who would never think to make a prejudicial remark when it comes to race, religion or gender, but they will make very hurtful remarks about how stupid those "other folks" (those of the opposite political persuasion) are. The problem comes in when people are so sure that they are right, that they don't even realize they're being mean and they don't realize that people that they admire for other reasons could possibly think differently about political issues.

So what I'd like guidance about is how to raise people's awareness that the SpeakStrong rules apply even for political discussions, and even when they think they're only with people of similar viewpoints.

Meryl responds:
I agree that they are probably unaware that their words are unkind and that there is someone listening who doesn't share their opinions. You are already a step ahead of the game with that insight. Once we become sensitive to the value of reasoned dialogue and the destructive nature of disparaging others, it's hurtful to listen to people revile others even when we generally agree.

Here are some phrases that you might find useful,
- *Are you aware that I'm one of those (idiots, stupid people etc.)? That you're actually talking about me?*
- *I actually hold different views than you do, but when you speak about (liberals/conservatives etc.) that way, I'm not sure it's safe to express my views.*
- *I know some people think those who disagree politically are fair game for personal attacks, but I'd like us to speak with the same respect we do about other races, genders and religions. You never know when one of those people you're calling stupid is the person you're talking to.*

You could also ignore the insult and address the issue as if they had expressed their opinion graciously.
- *I'm hoping that legislation passes.*
- *I'm as concerned about (issue) as they are.*
- *I think they have a point.*

That's less direct, but once you agree with or acknowledge the people they're slamming, chances are they'll get the idea and watch their words.

2. "The other side"

Meryl,
I'd like to know how to respond to someone who sends me information so that I can "see how the other side feels/thinks." First, I find it insulting as it assumes that I don't. Their opinion being that if I listened to the other side, I'd agree with them.

This topic is not only relevant given today's political scene, but I've just been having a difficult email dialogue with my only sister/sibling. Since she doesn't feel as well-informed (nor wants to be, really) enough to discuss any political topic intelligently, she had a friend espouse her views for her, which made me feel doubly insulted. I was careful about how I responded, but I'm still a bit heated. At this point, I think we've agreed to disagree.

Meryl responds:

First, let's look at the fallacy in her comment and the assumptions you make.

For starters, the term "the other side" is a fallacy. It sets up a false dichotomy, implying there are two monolithic groups, and if you talk to one member of either group, you've talked to them all. It erases individual differences. It sets you up for Divide and Conquer.

Second, you assume motive in her request. You may well be correct about that, but I suggest you explore your assumptions. It appears to me that you're assuming:
1) They assume you don't have an understanding of what others think.

2) If you have the benefit of their wisdom, you'll agree.

If those assumptions are accurate, they might indicate another false dichotomy – there are two sides to every story – theirs (the right one) and yours (the wrong one.)

While I agree it's unusual, I don't regard having someone else dialogue for her to be insulting to you. It could even be a compliment – that she feels inadequate to meet you one on one. Involving someone else makes it less personal, but it could make her arguments more accurate, which would be useful if you are interested in meaningful exchange.

It sounds like you have decided you already know everything they have to say, and they have already decided your opinions are not only wrong, but not worth considering. I don't hear any hint of collaboration, mutual curiosity or desire for clarification from either of you.

So first, you both have to decide if you want to engage or not. Unless you redefine your purposes in speaking, I don't hold out much hope for genuine communication.

If you are interested in genuine dialogue, say:

> *I'd like for us to shift from adversaries to collaborators. I'd like to change the tone of our conversations to one of openness. I'd like to be able to influence you and I'm open to being influenced by you. Are you open to that?*

You can invite your sister's proxy into the process as well. Then remember to look for common ground and say what you mean and mean what you say without being mean when you say it.

Of course, you do have the option to say,
> *I haven't found our political conversations to be productive. I'd rather keep our conversations non-political.*

3. Alternative opinions
The only right perspective:
Meryl,
Thank you for your always enlightening newsletter. I would like to know how to respectfully say "your opinion isn't the only/right opinion." And I would really like the person to "get it." Hope you can help.

Meryl responds:
Reflect back the words that led you to conclude they are opinionated, the way it comes across and the implications of it. For example, say:
- *I'm hearing you suggest that questioning this policy is a travesty and anyone who does that is an immoral idiot. Is that what you're saying?*
- *So are you suggesting that if I don't see it as you do, that I am an idiot?*

If they answer yes, you probably don't have much to work with, but I'd give it another try. Say:
> *I question this policy for what I think are very substantive reasons. I'd like to discuss them logically if you're willing.*

Or you could ignore the dig and simply respond by saying:
> *I think about this differently: here is my opinion on that topic.*

You may not be able to get through, but it's worth a try.

<u>Many alienated people:</u>
Meryl,
I think one of the most common occurrences we run into is the situation where someone we genuinely like begins the tirade concerning politics and their thoughts are the only valid opinions out there! My best friend is so certain that her opinion is the only "righteous" opinion and she becomes extremely verbally violent. If you propose to offer another opinion you immediately become an uneducated idiot.

Because she sooooooooo strongly believes that hers is the only correct opinion, I make a point of NEVER discussing politics or religion. I have made the decision that if this continues (and I'm sure it will as elections are still a long way off!) I am just going to tell her that I will not have this discussion because she makes me feel as if I am not intelligent enough to have my own opinions. She has alienated many people because she is so opinionated.

Meryl responds:
First, draw a general boundary about verbal violence as unacceptable in your relationship. Say:

That kind of language has no place in our friendship and I will not tolerate it. I'd like to continue this discussion, but not in this way.

Second, apply the suggestions I offered in my previous post.

Third, ask for the kind of dialogue you want. Say:

> *I'd like to exchange ideas with you about politics, but only if we can find ways to do that respectfully. I'd like for us to learn from each other. Are you open to seeing how we can do that?*

If you can't, then by all means, set your boundaries – even if it means saying:

> *Stop! This is inappropriate!*

And walking out of the room when necessary.

4. False "facts"
Meryl,
How can I tell someone the "facts" they base their opinion on are incorrect in a way that will open them to checking it out?

Meryl responds:
Say:
- *I am aware that there are people perpetuating that claim, but I have researched it and it's not true.*
- *What is your source for that information? Have you found them to be credible?*

- *I'd like to dialogue with you, but the information you base your opinion on has been discredited. If you're willing to check your facts with more neutral sources, we can continue. Otherwise I'd rather stop debating facts and start researching them.*

They might be more committed to their information than to finding the truth, in which case I suggest you refuse to dialogue unless/until they open to verifying their claims.

> **"It ain't what you don't know that gets you into trouble. It's what you know for sure that just ain't so." ~ Mark Twain**

5. Beyond bad taste
Meryl,
Often "opinions" veer over the line of what I can tolerate, even in an "agree to disagree" discussion. At a gathering recently, at a friend's home, my husband and I were both in a small group of individuals discussing a variety of things, when one member of the group began making radical political comments, suggesting extreme legislation targeting certain minorities. He proceeded to make derogatory comments about our hosts for their political views.

I was insulted by his behavior; I told him I disagreed with his opinion and found his comments about our hosts in very bad taste. I said it was his choice not to be around persons of color if he felt this way, but it was rude to accept hospitality and then insult them in their own home. I also stated it was my choice not to be in the presence of someone who would make those kinds of remarks. I said I was going to do what I felt he should have, and remove myself from the situation. I walked away and avoided his presence for the rest of the evening.

I didn't want to offend my hosts with my behavior to one of their guests (they are good friends) and they have known this individual for quite some time, but I felt his comments were over the top of common courtesy. I do know that others in the group that heard him were also uncomfortable, but everyone else chose to ignore it. So, please tell me if there was a better way to have handled this?

Meryl responds:
It sounds to me like you handled it well. You were clear, kind and direct.

One suggestion I would offer is that you might have inquired about your understanding before coming to conclusions. Even if it's almost beyond question that he was being as abrasive as you concluded, you might have said:

> *I'm wondering if I'm hearing you correctly, because it sounds like you're in favor of legislation that is based on hate toward our host's race. I'm aghast and wonder if one of us is missing something.*

It's interesting that others were also uncomfortable, but you were the only one willing to speak up. My hope is some day we will have well-accepted and effective guidelines for bystander behavior. Your comment is a model for new behavior.

I would be curious to know if he tones his rhetoric down in the future.

6. Chain email

Meryl,

The day after the 2007 anniversary of 9/11, I got a chain email from one of my cousins, which I could immediately tell was pure propaganda. I hate, hate, hate chain email. Someone in my extended family sends out a chain email every month or so, which annoys me. Why people can't write out their own opinions and thoughts, rather than just forward some unsubstantiated crap, I can't understand.

Anyway, when I read the chain email something about the email just got to me. My cousin is usually pretty rational, but I really wanted to just shout out to all my family to just stop being so thick headed. I did a quick Google of the article they forwarded and found that the story had multiple major errors. Why would anyone half-way smart sent out such a piece of propaganda (filled with lies, and using very emotional and strong photos from 9/11), which was just meant to falsely bash a politician who isn't even in office anymore? This just doesn't seem rational.

My thought at the time was "Don't use lies to make your point! You want to debate. Let's debate with the facts. I don't stoop so low as to use lies and people's deaths to make bogus political points (at least, I sure hope I don't. If I do, you have every right to yell at me, too). I expect my family to be smarter than that. Stupid people don't belong in my family. Well, I know I can't respond that way, so what should I say?

Meryl responds:
I suggest you welcome them as an opportunity to create clarity. Write something like:

> *Thanks for sending this. It's useful to know what's circulating the internet and what information you're reading. It helps me understand why some people form the opinions they do.*
>
> *I researched this email and found it perpetuates misinformation. Instead of detailing how, I'll refer you to (Snopes, etc.)*
>
> *Also, I find the emotional tone of the email exploitive. Starting with the twin towers pictures, putting an exclamation point after "It was 1987!" the all caps and the "do not break the chain" admonition at the end seem designed to overshadow reason with emotion.*
>
> *I find you to be a rational thinker, so I'm confused that you might have found this credible. What do you value in the email? I'd love to dialogue about the facts and I invite you to share your thoughts and opinions.*
>
> *And keep me on the list when you send forwards. I'd like to use them to help us dialogue accurately and personally about our share.*

I would think this would result in them being more careful with their forwards in the future. However, if you definitely don't want to receive any more forwards, say:

I researched your email forward and found it to be full of inaccuracies. Please either verify your emails before forwarding, or delete me from your list.

I hope you choose to research the accuracy of your emails because I think it is destructive to circulate misinformation.

Thanks!

Kudos to you for taking the time to respond and clarify.

Chapter 21

Some boats need to be rocked

Most of us don't like rocking the boat. But some boats need to be rocked. Here are a few.

> *"A lie can get halfway around the world before the truth can even get its boots on." ~ Mark Twain*

<u>Rock the trivial correctness boat</u>

Political correctness can be very incorrect. It can distract from a much bigger issue. Some things are worth championing with a passion. If you stay silent out of political correctness to avoid rocking the boat, you are incorrect in your correctness.

While you fervently make nice and act polite, others who don't have the same restraint will be drowning out the voice of reason. Knee-jerk reactionary voices steer policy when the voices of reason stay silent.

Edmund Burke is credited with saying, "All that's necessary for the forces of evil to win in the world is for enough good men to do nothing."

Some boats need to be rocked.

Rock the apathy boat

If anyone tells you they don't care about politics, rock the boat. Saying you don't care about politics is like saying you don't care about how you are allowed to live, what you're taxed on and how your taxes are spent. It's like writing a blank check and letting someone else decide who gets to spend it. It's like letting your neighbor decide who you should grant power of attorney over your affairs to.

Rock the political apathy boat wherever you see it. Ask what they figure is more important.

Rock the futility boat

If people tell you there's no point in participating in the political process because nothing will ever change, rock the boat. Saying political participation is futile is a self-fulfilling prophecy. If enough people say it's futile to participate in politics, it will be. Democracy depends on an informed engaged populace. Become a constructive citizen.

Despair is not an option. We overcome despair with action. Simple actions, speaking up for open, logical dialogue move all of us forward.

Rock the unknowable boat

If people tell you the spin is so thick the truth is unknowable, rock the boat. It is difficult to separate truth from spin, but not impossible. Sometimes it's a matter of reading the entire article instead of just the misleading headline. Information is readily available now. Make use of it.

If enough people decide truth is unknowable, liars can operate in the cover of darkness. They don't have to convince anyone they're right, they just have to create doubt. That sets the bar very low. The unknowable boat provides a pass for those who don't want the truth known and punishes those who fight for truth and justice by casting the shadow of doubt over them.

Rock the misinformation boat

If people spread misinformation or decline to challenge it, rock the boat. You don't have to spread misinformation yourself to be complicit in its proliferation. The disseminators of disinformation have motivation to spread propaganda and lies. They could never succeed if people who know better spread accurate information with the same enthusiasm.

The next time you receive a bogus email, send *corrections* to 30 of your closest friends.

> *"I was brought up to believe that the only thing worth doing was to add to the sum of accurate information in the world." ~ Margaret Mead*

Rock the immediate gratification boat

If people are more concerned with their immediate needs than the long term implications of actions, rock the boat. Corporations operate with their eyes on the next quarter earnings. Politicians operate with an eye on the next election. And too many citizens figure as long as the television is working and there's beer in the fridge, everything is fine.

Some Native American tribes based their decisions on the impact the decision would have on the next seven generations. Accept their wisdom. Rock the short-term thinking, immediate gratification boat. Be an advocate for long-term considerations.

Rock the "they're all the same" boat
If people suggest it makes no difference who's in power, rock the boat. You might not get everything you think you want from anyone, but it does matter.

If people suggest the truth lies halfway in between two positions, rock the boat. After all, if a serial killer and an anointed saint were in a debate, you would know the truth is NOT half-way in between. We may not like our choices, but we have them.

Rock the verbal anarchy boat
If people ignore guidelines for reasoned discourse, rock the boat. Advocate for honest arguments that seek the truth, not verbal anarchy that wins arguments at any cost.

Rock the "it's not my problem" boat (the one that's docked next to the "apathy" boat)
If people suggest that something done in their name is "not my problem," rock the boat. If you don't participate, you are complicit in what happens, and it IS your problem. This is our country and we need to take ownership.

*"Where respect says 'Don't hurt', responsibility
says 'Do help'." ~ Thomas Lickona*

Rock the "we can't talk about that" boat

If people label a topic as off limits, rock the boat. A relationship is as healthy as the things you can talk about. So is a nation. The things you don't want to talk about are probably exactly the things you need to talk about.

Strong ideas should be able to stand up to examination. When people argue that a topic should not even be raised, it could be an indication that this is a topic that needs to be raised, because it is unlikely to stand up to scrutiny.

Rock the "I don't want to rock the boat" boat

If you or anyone doesn't want to rock the boat, rock the boat. Some boats need to be rocked. If you don't rock it, people with a less benevolent agenda will. Be strategic about what boats you rock and how you rock them, but never ever shy away from rocking a boat that needs to be rocked now.

*"We only fully trust a relation if it has
survived occasional conflict"
~ Frans De Waal*

*"History will have to record that the greatest tragedy of
this period of social transition was not the
strident clamor of the bad people, but the
appalling silence of the good people."
~ Martin Luther King*

Meryl Runion

Chapter 22

Stop arguing, start communicating

The voices they don't hear

It sounded straightforward to me. A congresswoman wrote she received calls from lobbyists and extremists, but she rarely heard from constituents about standing up to those forces. She advocated calling our "congresscritters" to offer the input and offer support they rarely get.

She suggested we call and politely say, *Please represent us in the following ways. I will back you up if you do. I will write letters to the editor, whatever is needed to show that you have my support.*

She went on to say, *Doing this is the only way we'll see change.*

I didn't see anything to argue with. I was stunned that 50 commenters did.

They should know

Most of the blog commenters complained that calling our congressmen is futile and "should" be unnecessary because they *should* know.

Yeah, and my husband *should* know what to get me for Christmas, but my chances of getting it are far greater if I ask.

The fringes speak loudly, unreasonably and passionately. The middle needs to speak clearly, reasonably and every bit as passionately.

Special interests speak loudly, unreasonably and with money. Reasonable people need to speak clearly, reasonably and in large numbers.

The resistance to what seemed like straightforward advice took me aback. The commenters seemed more interested in complaining and tearing down than advocating and encouraging their representatives protect the interest of citizen over extreme interests.

If the responses on the blog are an accurate indication of the state of our political dialogue with each other, and with our leaders, it's clear how dysfunctional it is.

People don't know what you want unless you tell them – in a way they can hear.

Speak Strong
There's an alternative to being passive other than being aggressive. There's an alternative to being aggressive other than being passive. I call it Speaking Strong, which I define as saying what you mean without being mean when you say it. Be brief, be specific and target your words for results.

Just because the national political dialogue is insane, doesn't mean yours should be.

Just because pundits and politicians act like anyone who disagrees has declared war, doesn't mean you should.

Just because the game of "gotcha" plays out on our airwaves, doesn't mean it should play out in your home, neighborhood or office. And...

Just because someone in your life thinks manners are obsolete when a conversation gets political, doesn't mean you have to take what they dish out.

It's time to have a serious dialogue about reasonable dialogue.

Be an Accuracy Advocate and a Passionate Voice of Reason

The opportunities to be an Accuracy Advocate and a passionate Voice of Reason are endless. Here are nine:

1. Speak up when show hosts use fallacies in their political arguments. Call or email and request that they speak with accuracy.
2. Speak up when people send you inaccurate and inappropriate emails. Send corrections and ask them to pass the corrections on to everyone they sent the original emails to.
3. Speak up when people bully or intimidate people into silence. Insist they treat everyone with respect.
4. Speak up when dialogue moves away from the issues into personal attack. Bring the focus back to the substantive issues.

5. Speak up when blog posts turn nasty. Redirect the conversation away from mudslinging toward rational dialogue.

6. Suggest, request and insist that blog owners set standards for posts. Let them know that you want substance, not flames.

7. Talk about the things that matter to you. Make political dialogue a proper conversation for "polite company."

8. Change the way you communicate with your congressional representatives. Let them know what you want, and applaud them when they represent you the way you want them to. Meet them in person whenever you can.

9. Get involved with a political party. If your party no longer represents you, get involved and advocate rational dialogue.

"In politics, a lie unanswered becomes truth within 24 hours." ~ Willie Brown

Stop reacting and start interacting

An amazing thing happens when you stop reacting. Walls that seemed impenetrable dissolve. Situations that once seemed explosive are defused. Problems that were once insolvable are addressed.

Whether it's by choice or design, we really are all in this together. It's time we start acting like we are.

Now it is time to get out there and Restore Sanity to Political Conversation. Stop arguing, and start communicating about politics. Tag. You're it. Democracy begins with you.

Appendix

I.

Glittering generalities, name-calling words and reframing

Former Speaker of the House Newt Gingrich was an influential advocate of political abstraction and verbal labeling. His political action committee (GOPAC) mailed a pamphlet entitled *Language, A Key Mechanism of Control* to Republicans across the country. The booklet offered rhetorical advice to Republican candidates who wanted to "speak like Newt."

The National Conference of Teachers of English awarded his pamphlet a Doublespeak Award in 1990.

The booklet contained a list of "positive, governing words (glittering generalities)" to use when speaking about themselves, and a second set of negative words (name-calling words) to use against their opponents.

Glittering generalities
This is the list of "positive, governing words" that GOP candidates were told to use when speaking about themselves or their policies.

Active(ly), Activist, Building, Candid(ly), Care(ing), Challenge, Change, Children, Choice/choose, Citizen, Commitment, Common sense, Compete, Confident, Conflict, Control, Courage, Crusade, Debate, Dream, Duty, Eliminate good-time in prison, Empower(ment),

Environment, Fair, Family, Freedom, Hard work, Help, Humane, Incentive, Initiative, Lead, Learn, Legacy, Liberty, Light, Listen, Mobilize, Moral, Movement, Opportunity, Passionate, Peace, Pioneer, Precious, Premise, Preserve, Principle(d), Pristine, Pro-(issue) (flag,) (children,) (environment,) Prosperity, Protect, Proud/pride, Provide Reform Rights Share Strength Success Tough Truth Unique Vision We/us/our Workfare

Name-calling words
This is the list of negative words and phrases that GOP candidates were told to use when speaking about their opponents.

"Compassion" is not enough, Anti-(issue) flag, family, child, jobs, Betray, Coercion, Collapse, Consequences, Corruption, Crisis, Decay, Deeper, Destroy, Destructive, Devour, Endanger, Failure, Greed, Hypocrisy, Ideological, Impose, Incompetent, Insecure, Liberal, Lie, Limit(s), Pathetic, Permissive attitude, Radical, Self-serving, Sensationalists, Shallow, Sick, They/them, Threaten, Traitors, Unionized bureaucracy, Urgent, Waste

When I present these lists at seminars, a common response from attendees is: "that sounds familiar." Clearly Gingrich's lists had a powerful influence on the national political dialogue that continues almost 20 years later.

More wordsmithing
A more recent example of political wordsmithing and languaging can be found in pollster Frank Luntz's Republican Playbook. You can read it online at:

http://www.politicalstrategy.org/archives/001185.php

You'll find Luntz's language familiar as well. Here are some of Luntz's rewrites.
- From global warming to: climate change
- From tax cuts to: tax relief
- From war in Iraq to: war on terror
- From offshore drilling to: deep sea energy exploration
- From drilling for oil to: exploring for energy
- From wiretapping or eavesdropping to: electronic intercepts
- From minority party to: opposition party
- From philosophy to: ideas
- From school vouchers to: opportunity scholarships
- From timber industry bill to: Healthy Forests Initiative
- From Social Security privatization to: Social Security personalization

According to Frontline, "Frank Luntz has built his career on a simple idea: "It doesn't matter what you want to tell the public -- it's about what they want to hear."

II.

Attacks / Counterattacks

The search for influential wordsmiths on the Democratic side yields fewer and lesser-known results. Most of what you do find is defensive – more about rejecting the GOP definitions than creating powerful new ways of talking about what the left believes in.

http://jeffrey-feldman.typepad.com/

One Democratic wordsmith is linguist George Lakoff. Lakoff's primary message to the political left has been to use their own language rather than repeating wording provided by the GOP.

Here is a web post by Lakoff which answers the question: *How can we respond to conservative attacks on our patriotism?*

> We were asked how to respond when confronted with the attack, "Aw you liberals just hate America."
>
> This is name-calling with a destructive (and false) frame. There are times when it is necessary to have a retort, not for its own sake, but to allow you to shift the frame and say a lot more on any one of many topics. The replacement frame should express <u>progressive views</u> while revealing key truths hidden by the original frame. Here is one strategy:
>
> **"Aw you liberals just hate America."**
> No. We love democracy and we want to return it to America.

You want a presidential dictator.
We love liberty and we want to return it to America.
You want to tap our phones.
We love equality and we want to return it to America.
You think some people are better than others.
We love honesty and we want to return it to America.
You love lobbyists and corruption.
We love fairness and we want to return it to America.
You want to oppress the powerless.
We love openness and we want to return it to America.
You love secrecy and hiding the facts.
We love nature's glory and we want to return it to America.
You love the profit that comes from destroying nature.
We love community and we want to return it to America.
You want everyone to fend for himself.
We love public education and we want to return it to America.
You want to destroy public education.
We love civilian control of the military and we want to return it to America.
You want to militarize America.
And on and on...

Source: George Lakoff, The Rockridge Institute)

I can't imagine that kind of reductionism and labeling will convince anyone.

Let's take a look at the accusations. The remark: "You liberals hate America" contains more fallacies than words.

1. Absolute language: It speaks of liberals as if they're all alike.

2. Reductive: It summarizes a complex situation simplistically.

3. Ad hominen attack: It attacks the person instead of the person's position

4. Argues abstraction: Hating America can mean anything.

5. More absolute language: It speaks of hating America as an absolute.

6. Mind reading: It projects an attitude of hate.

Lakoff's initial response: "No. We love democracy and we want to return it to America" makes the discussion slightly more concrete and provides a modicum of clarity, but the retort: "You want a presidential dictator" is as inflammatory as the initial attack, and likely to polarize the discussion further.

Instead of responding to an abstraction with another abstraction, and responding to a personal attack with a counterattack, refocus the discussion to make it more concrete. Say:

> *Let's not get personal here. I'm an individual, not a political leaning, and I expressed an objection to policy X. I'd like to know why you support policy X. Whether or not I'm patriotic has nothing to do with the merits of this policy.*

See how handy logic is?

III.

Glossary

Absolute language

Absolute language is dominating language. Absolute talkers define issues in black and white terms and do not acknowledge the existence of subtleties. Absolute language creates a false-choice-dichotomy which distracts the listener from considering alternatives. That limits the debate to alternatives suggested by the absolute thinker. If someone asks if I prefer Coke or Pepsi, I may not consider the options of water or carrot juice

Accuracy Advocate

Accuracy Advocates speak up for precision and truth. Not only do they check information for accuracy before they pass it on, they let those who propagate false information know that their information is faulty, and request a higher standard of accuracy for future dialogue.

Aggression's Law

Aggression's Law is my adaptation of the economic concept called Gresham's Law. Aggressions' Law says that erroneous arguments drown out accurate ones. Unprincipled diatribe drives out reason. She who is most ruthlessly committed to prevail wins, regardless of the validity of her arguments.

Argumentum ad hominen

Argumentum ad hominen attacks the messenger instead of addressing the argument. That distracts from the logic of an argument by challenging their qualifications to make the argument.

Argumentum ad populum

(everyone agrees, bandwagon, tyranny of the majority)

Argumentum ad populum suggests that because a concept is popular, it must be true. Instead of addressing an idea on its merits, it considers endorsements as proof.

Argumentum ad Misericordiam

(Argument from pity, appeal to emotion)

Argumentum ad Misericordiam suggests that someone's opinion is valid because they deserve empathy. Argumentum ad Misericordiam is one of many appeals to emotion. Other appeals to emotion are appeal to guilt, shame, fear, anger, etc.

Brainlet

Our brains consist of three brain systems – the Reptilian, Mammalian and Neocortical Brain Systems. I call the brainlets because it's much friendlier than the phrase "brain system."

Complement

Not opposition. Effective communication involves the discovery and consideration of things in common.

Concerned Citizen

A concerned citizen takes ownership of democracy and considers it their responsibility to play a role in making our shared government work. In this book I refer to a Concerned Citizen as someone who consciously plays a role in raising the effectiveness and civility of dialogue.

Concur

Concur means to work cooperatively to reach a meeting of the minds. It involves regarding the people in our lives as partners in trying to determine the truth and best course of action.

Debate

Debate means to engage in argument by discussing opposing points. The root is from debatre, to fight, contend, to beat down. Debate is based on the idea of opposition and contest.

Deception Detective

A Deception Detective is someone who had developed a trained, critical ear and uncovers fallacies, distortions and false logic.

Derailed conversation

A derailed conversation is one that loses track of its initial purpose. Conversations are derailed when people are triggered into Reptilian Regressions, Mammalian Meltdowns and Neocortical Apartheids and when assumptions override inquiry.

Dialogue

A conversation between two or more people that involves an exchange of ideas or opinions. It comes from the root: Dia Logus: "Through Words." Dialogue involves equality among participants and involves the exchange of idea.

Diatribe

Diatribe is a bitter, sharply abusive denunciation, attack, or criticism. It comes from the Greek root: diatribē, pastime, lecture, and from diatrībein, to consume, wear away. And that's what it does.

Dichotomy

Dichotomy divides ideas and possibilities into two mutually exclusive, opposed, or contradictory groups. Dichotomy polarizes, separates and ignores subtleties.

Disempowerment

You disempower someone when you deprive them of influence and importance. In conversation, one party might disempower the other by judging or dismissing them.

Domination

Domination exercises control over another. In conversation, a dominator will apply pressure and other tactics to ensure that their opinions take precedence regardless of the merit or lack of merit of their arguments.

Fact Fanatic

A Fact Fanatic is committed to communicating based on substance and reality. Instead of accepting and passing on nonsense, they appraise the credibility of claims.

Fallacy Finder

A Fallacy Finder is skilled in observing and identifying logical fallacies. They use this skill to return the dialogue to a reasonable one.

Glittering generalities

Glittering generalities are a list of "positive, governing words" that GOP candidates were told to use when speaking about themselves or their policies.

In complement

I use the term "in complement" as an antonym to the phrase "in common." In common refers to similarities. In complement indicates differences in a way that suggests you complete each other.

Izzie

The Reptilian Brainlet. I named it Izzie because I use a stuffed lizard to represent that brainlet that was named Izzie by the manufacturer. (Sadly, Izzie has been discontinued.)

Mammalian Meltdown

What happens when the Webby, mammalian brainlet dominates, overshadowing input from the reptilian or neocortical brainlet.

Neocortical Apartheid

This is the term I use for when the neocortical brainlet (The Prof) isolates and ignores input from the reptilian and mammalian brainlet.

Personalization

The victim personalizer treats challenges to ideas as personal attacks. The bully personalizer attacks the character or qualifications of the commenter. Both personalizers avoid addressing issues on their own merit.

PowerPhrase

A short, specific, targeted phrase that says what you mean and means what you say without being mean when you say it.

The Prof

This is the neocortical, intellectual brain.

Reptilian Regression

When the primal, reptilian brainlet dominates, I call it a Reptilian Regression.

Serenity Affirmation

The Serenity Affirmation is an adaptation of the Serenity Prayer for secular applications. It states: "I have the serenity to accept the things I cannot change, the courage to change the things I can and the wisdom to know the difference."

Slippery slope (runaway train, overall generalization)

Slippery slope arguments suggest that a small step in any direction will lead to planetary destruction and/or global depravity. It argues that the first step must be avoided to avoid the extreme outcome.

Snopes

Snopes is one of the better known and most trusted urban myth evaluation resources. www.snopes.com

SpeakStrong

What you do when you say what you mean, and mean what you say, without being mean when you say it.

Straw man argument

Straw man arguments misrepresent the other's position in ways that are easy to dispute, and then argue against that manufactured claim or request that no one actually makes.

Synergnyms

A word I created to suggest a balance between two extremes.

Systems problem

Systems problems are problems that result from flawed systems rather than the actions individuals who are trying to implement the flawed system.

Third-wit

When one of your three brains dominates, you are operating as a "third-wit."

Triune Brain

The theory that our brain consists of three brains that develop in sequence. The primal reptilian brainlet is the first to develop, the emotional mammalian brainlet is the second and the intellectual neocortical brainlet is the third.

Truth Sleuth

The Truth Sleuth listens openly to what others say with the intent to separate spin from substance.

Unwarranted

Something unwarranted is unjustifiable and superfluous. An unwarranted assumption is an assumption that others don't share.

Voice of Reason

A person who is the Voice of Reason advocates for reasonable dialogue.

Webby

I nicknamed the mammalian, emotional brain Webby because the name starts with the word "we" and creates connections.

Yeah but you

When people defensively throw arguments back at the person making them, I say they're Yeah-but-you-ing them. I also refer to the tactic as examining the speck in your eye when you want to discuss the beam in theirs.

IV.

Communicating empowerment as we speak

We use several distinct styles of spoken communication and each one communicates the power stance of the relationship along with the semantics of the message. In every communication there are two messages, one about the semantics of the discussion, the other about the relationship of the participants. The following table distinguishes between dialogue, discussion, debate, delegation, dogma and other terms we use to describe spoken communications. Peers are equals and they collaborate using dialogue. It is the only symmetrical form of communication. The other forms establish or reinforce asymmetrical, power-based relationships.

Term	Definition	Power Stance	Example
Dialogue	A conversation between two or more people. An exchange of ideas or opinions. Root: Dia Logus, "Through Words" Dialogue requires both talk and silence to create an interweaving of ideas.	We are peers, collaborating to solve a problem we are facing together. Let's work together to discover an understanding. Your views are essential to solving the problem. Completely open to new ideas — Cooperation.	Typical of the best scientific inquiry and collaboration. "What is the best design for our new product?"
Discussion	Consideration of a subject by a group. Talk or writing in which the pros and cons of a subject are considered. Root: same as Percussion, "ping pong," back and forth, offense and defense.	I am scoring points against your arguments. Your point of view will eventually come around. Somewhat open to new ideas — Consideration.	A typical conversation that begins by expressing a point of view or suggesting a solution, rather than stating a problem or need. "May I bounce my new design off of you?"
Debate	To engage in argument by discussing opposing points. Root: from debatre, to fight, contend, to beat down.	I am right, you are wrong, your way of thinking is incorrect, the facts you present are incorrect. Your point of view is wrong. You need to submit to my better judgment. Not open to new ideas — Contention.	Presidential debates: "I am clearly the best candidate." "No, I am clearly the best candidate." Development: "This is the best design." Marketing: "We can't afford to wait so long for you to build it."

Term	Definition	Power Stance	Example
Defend	To ward off an attack. Root: from défendere to ward off.	Notice if the defense is primarily evidence based or power based. An evidence based defense endorses the facts, a power based one doubts the facts.	The earth is estimated to be approximately 4 billion years old based on the following evidence gathered by geologists, paleontologists, and astronomers: . . .
Distraction	Diverting attention. Root: Latin distrahere, distract-, to pull away	I don't care to respond to you and you don't have the power to make me respond.	Bloviation, obfuscation, restating the question, changing the subject . . .
Dismissal	To discard or reject. Root: dis- + mittere, to send.	You are not worth engaging in any further discussion. — Contempt.	How dare you ask? If you don't even know that, I can't help you.
Delegation	To assign work and responsibility to someone else. Root: from delegatus, to appoint.	I have power and you don't. What I want and need are important, your needs are not. Why don't you just keep quiet or do it yourself — Control.	"I think it would be great if we had a department picnic." "Great idea, why don't you plan it. "Development: "How do you expect us to meet that deadline?" Management: That's what I hired you to figure out."
Disingenuous	Not straightforward or candid; insincere or calculating. Not genuine.	You are not worth communicating with honestly and genuinely. . . and we both know there is nothing you can do about it.	The recorded message that repeats "Your call is important to us" as you are kept on hold endlessly.

217

Term	Definition	Power Stance	Example
Dialectic	Tension and synthesis of opposites. Root: from Latin dialectica, logic, from Greek dialektikē, the art of debate	Done best when wise, respectful, and vigorous peers adopt the stance of: my viewpoint and logic is as valid as yours.	This can be very useful to stimulate thinking and explore the creative tension of naturally occurring conflicts, such as between speed and accuracy or the aspirations of hope and the stubbornness of evidence.
Decree	An authoritative order having the force of law. Root: from dēcernere, to decide.	I have chosen to exercise my positional power and make this final decision.	Court judgments or executive decisions and pronouncements.
Diatribe	A bitter, sharply abusive denunciation, attack, or criticism Root: from Greek diatribē, pastime, lecture, from diatrībein, to consume, wear away	I know the Truth and I will lecture you forcefully, self-righteously, and angrily until you understand.	
Dogma	An authoritative principle, belief, or statement of ideas or opinion, especially one considered to be absolute truth. Root: dogma, that which one thinks true, a decree	I have the power, you do not. This is truth. Do this. Do not debate or discuss. Comply or else. There is no other point of view. Completely closed to new ideas — Conformance, submission.	"The earth is the center of the universe." And "we've always done it this way."

V.

Resources

Here are a few resources you can use to check information for accuracy:

www.factcheck.org
Fact-check.org is a nonpartisan, nonprofit, "consumer advocate" for voters that aims to reduce the level of deception and confusion in U.S. politics. They monitor the factual accuracy of what major U.S. political players say in TV ads, debates, speeches, interviews, and news releases. Their goal is to apply the best practices of both journalism and scholarship, and to increase public knowledge and understanding.

The Annenberg Political Fact Check is a project of the Annenberg Public Policy Center of the University of Pennsylvania. The APPC was established by publisher and philanthropist Walter Annenberg in 1994 to create a community of scholars within the University of Pennsylvania that would address public policy issues at the local, state, and federal levels.

The APPC accepts no funding from business corporations, labor unions, political parties, lobbying organizations or individuals. It is funded primarily by the Annenberg Foundation.

www.snopes.com
Snopes aims to debunk or confirm widely spread urban legends, including political ones. News media and other sites refer to Snopes as evidence of accuracy or inaccuracy of reports. Some chain e-mail hoaxes falsely claim that to have been "checked out on 'Snopes.com'" to discourage readers from seeking verification.

Where appropriate, pages are generally marked "undetermined" or "unverifiable" if the hosts feel there is not enough evidence to either support or disprove a given claim.

www.opensecrets.org

Opensecrets.org is the site for: The Center for Responsive Politics. CFRP is a non-partisan, non-profit research group based in Washington, D.C. that tracks money in politics, and its effect on elections and public policy. It's the place to go to find out which lobbyists support which candidates. The Center conducts computer-based research on campaign finance issues for the news media, academics, activists, and the public at large. The Center's work is aimed at creating a more educated voter, an involved citizenry, and a more responsive government.

Support for the Center comes from a combination of foundation grants and individual contributions. The Center accepts no contributions from businesses or labor unions.

www.cbo.gov

The Congressional Budget Office, or CBO's mandate is to provide the Congress with:

- Objective, nonpartisan, and timely analyses to aid in economic and budgetary decisions on the wide array of programs covered by the federal budget, and,

- The information and estimates required for the Congressional budget process.

www.gao.gov

The U.S. Government Accountability Office (GAO) is known as "the investigative arm of Congress" and "the congressional watchdog." GAO supports the Congress in meeting its constitutional responsibilities. It helps improve the performance and ensure the accountability of the federal government for the benefit of the American people. GAO's work includes oversight of federal programs; insight into ways to make government more efficient, effective, ethical and equitable; and foresight of long-term trends and challenges.

www.guardian.co.uk

The Guardian is a British newspaper that was founded in 1821 and has a long history of editorial and political independence. It's reports provide an alternative view of international news.

www.ft.com/home/europe

Financial Times:

The Financial Times is a British financial newspaper that offers an alternative perspective to US financial news reports.